Cristiane de Carvalho Guimarães

Cartography of mental health care

Cristiane de Carvalho Guimarães

Cartography of mental health care

Rio de Janeiro

ScienciaScripts

Cover image: Provided by the author

This book is a translation from the original published under ISBN 978-620-2-03127-1.

Publisher:
Sciencia Scripts
is a trademark of
Dodo Books Indian Ocean Ltd. and OmniScriptum S.R.L publishing group

120 High Road, East Finchley, London, N2 9ED, United Kingdom
Str. Armeneasca 28/1, office 1, Chisinau MD-2012, Republic of Moldova, Europe
Printed at: see last page
ISBN: 978-620-8-35375-9

Presentation

In this book we will present the results of research carried out in Brazil. This research could only be carried out because at the beginning of the 1980s, participants in social movements, together with progressive parliamentarians, took on the task of confronting reactionary forces and proposed what has come to be known as the Brazilian Psychiatric Reform. This is a complex social process that involves changing the way people with mental disorders are cared for, in accordance with new technical and ethical assumptions, the cultural incorporation of these values and the legal validation of this new order. The Reform aims to build a new social status for people suffering from psychiatric disorders, which guarantees them citizenship, respect for their rights and their individuality, promoting their contractuality, the recovery of the individual's ability to participate in the universe of social exchanges, goods, words and affections.

The Psychiatric Reform is a process made up of actors, institutions and forces from different backgrounds, affecting different territories: federal, state and municipal governments, universities, the health services market, professional councils, associations of people with mental disorders and their families, social movements, and the territories of the social imagination and public opinion.

This process must be understood as a set of transformations in practices, knowledge, cultural and social values. And it is in the daily life of institutions, services and interpersonal relationships that it advances, marked by impasses, tensions, conflicts and challenges.

In the following pages, we will present texts that help to situate both the advances of Psychiatric Reform today, as well as some impasses that still need to be overcome.

In the first article, we take a look at the reality of emergency psychiatric care in Rio de Janeiro. The emergency room is one of the gateways to the Unified Health System (SUS), but it is currently vulnerable and unable to provide the care that the population needs. In this article we'll take a closer look at this situation.

In the second text, we can read the results of a qualitative, exploratory study carried out using bibliographic and documentary research techniques and observation of the Rio de Janeiro Psychiatric Center (CPRJ) and its current position in the mental health network in Rio de Janeiro. Since its creation, the CPRJ has maintained close ties with the community. It is an integrated service, with all types of care. It is a "small" mental health network. Since its creation in 1998, its fundamental and daily task has been to provide mental health care. The CPRJ is not an ideal service, resolutive in every sense (and perhaps such a service does not exist), but it is a service historically committed to building a new way of dealing with madness. There are spaces of coexistence inside and outside the CPRJ that are increasingly showing this possibility

In the third article, we present another study carried out at the Rio de Janeiro Psychiatric Center. Twenty interviews were conducted with users who had previous experience of psychiatric hospitalization(s). The answers to the questions about the future and the difference between hospitalization and HD stand out. The conclusion is that more research with users is needed and that the discussion of autonomy is a priority.

The fourth paper will discuss the importance of the Rio de Janeiro Psychiatric Center (CPRJ) by analyzing the relationship between users of CPRJ services and the community, their relationship with the mental health care network in the city and state of Rio de Janeiro. In this work, interviews were conducted with members of the community in order to analyze how they understand the insertion of users into society, given that the recovery of autonomy is one of the proposals of the Psychiatric Reform.

In the fifth and final paper, we will learn about the research carried out at Caps Jair Nogueira in Nova Iguagu, Rio de Janeiro, which aimed to analyze, through the narratives of its users, their perception of the effectiveness of the proposals made by the Psychiatric Reform and how they affect their lives. Listening to the mad. The conclusion is that although users prefer to be cared for in the Caps, the construction or reconstruction of their singularities is not the focus of the Singular Therapeutic Project and their plans for the future and their reinsertion or insertion into the community are still insipient. There is still a lot of work to be done if we are to build a new social place for the insane.

We understand psychiatric reform as a process. We can identify its beginning, but we cannot pinpoint its end. It is something that is being made, built and remade throughout history. There have certainly been many advances and major and serious setbacks, but the struggle is constant and just. So this work is like a photo, capturing a moment in a process. We invite you to dive into these texts and learn a little about this moment of psychiatric reform in Brazil.

Chapter 1

PSYCHIC SUFFERING NOT TREATED AS AN EMERGENCY

Renata Andrade Santos Pereira Amanda Milani de Oliveira Araujo
Rosane de Albuquerque Costa

INTRODUCTION

The Psychiatric Center of Rio de Janeiro (CPRJ) is a state public institution located in the city's port area. It has various types of service, such as a day hospital, crisis ward, outpatient clinic and emergency service, which operates 24 hours a day, seven days a week, as the gateway to the mental health care service (MINISTERIO DA SAUDE), which will be the central topic of discussion in this article. The CPRJ is part of one of the centers in Rio de Janeiro that still has a psychiatric emergency room, as well as housing the crisis treatment space (wards) and the day hospital in the same institution, which operate on completely opposite logics of care for individuals with psychic suffering. Since 2003, the SMS/RJ Regulation Center has been regulating the beds available in the institution, which welcomes not only users from its territory, but also from other municipalities in Rio de Janeiro (KAUSEN; CARVALHO, 2008).

The psychiatric emergency room plays a crucial role in the insertion and support of users in the public mental health system, making medication adjustments and assessing the general medical conditions associated with the psychiatric condition. Its purpose is to welcome and assess psychiatrists in order to provide better guidance, both for new cases and for those already in the network, with users being referred to outpatient services, Psychosocial Support Centers or, in acute cases, hospitalization, and replacing them when unavailable (DEL-BEN; TENG, 2010).

With the enactment of Law 10.216/01, which deals with mental health, protection and the rights of people with mental disorders and redirects the care model, psychiatric emergencies now have to be received by Psychiatric Units in General Hospitals, and then referred to continue treatment in specialized services. However, this is not currently the reality experienced by users of the mental health network. This is due to the low number of General Hospitals that have complied with the law, few of which have Psychiatric Units in the state of Rio de Janeiro. As such, this study seeks to contribute to the discussion of this issue in a meaningful way, promoting a look at the individual in psychiatric distress and their lack of support from health services when they are in crisis.

METHODOLOGY

The research was carried out at the Rio de Janeiro Psychiatric Center as an ethnography, in order to critically explore its emergency care over a period of four months (February, March, April and May). Observing the dynamics of its operation and the interaction established between patients and staff.

A bibliographic survey was carried out in the VHL (Virtual Health Library) database using the following descriptors: "Psychiatric Emergency", "Psychiatric Reform in Brazil" and "Reception in Public Health", in April 2015. The articles that were most relevant to the research theme were selected.

It was found that there are few articles on the subject in Brazil, thus corroborating the need for more research to be carried out in order to offer better care to users of psychiatric emergency services.

PSYCHIATRIC REFORM

Psychiatric reform originated in the late 1980s with the National Anti-Asylum Movement, which was made up of mental health workers, service users and their families. According to Prandonil, Padilha (2004) and Delgado (2011) this movement actively participated in the struggles for the inclusion of psychiatric patients in society and its motto was: "For a Society Without Asylums".

Deputy Paulo Delgado initiated the bill that institutionally legalized the psychiatric reform movement, which was approved by the Federal Chamber in 1989. But the law was only sanctioned by the President of the Republic on April 6, 2001. This gave rise to Law 10.216/01, which proposed the restructuring of psychiatric care in Brazil (PAULIN; TURATO, 2004).

Barros and Sales (2011) cite the main objectives of law 10.216/01, which are: to reduce low-quality psychiatric beds and strengthen the out-of-hospital network. Psychiatric reform proposes de-hospitalization by strengthening a community-based, out-of-hospital mental health care model, seeking to expand the network made up of Therapeutic Residence Services, Psychosocial Support Centres, Outpatient Mental Health Services and Psychiatric Units in General Hospitals. In addition to including the

Return Home Program, the policies for dealing with alcohol and other drug users and guaranteeing quality treatment for mentally ill offenders.

More than just guaranteeing the rights of people suffering from psychiatric illness, the Psychiatric Reform aims to bring a look of solidarity, understanding, respect and tolerance to madness, seeking to deconstruct the stigmas and stereotypes linked to it, as well as to the mentally ill (BEZERRA JR, 2007). In this way, the aim is for the insane person to be accepted by society as a citizen who is ill, but who can move freely around the city without posing any risk. The stigma of the dangerousness of madness needs to be urgently deconstructed from people's imaginations.

According to Delgado (2011), psychiatric reform is based on the principles of the SUS: universality, equity and comprehensiveness. It thus proposes that all people have the right to full care, close to their homes through territorialization, and that health facilities are integrated to meet the needs of their users. Hospitalization in any of its circumstances will only be indicated in accordance with law 10.216/01, when out-of-hospital resources prove insufficient, and will only be permitted on the basis of a medical report characterizing the reasons for it. (MINISTERIO DA SAUDE, 2001)

Currently, in the city of Rio de Janeiro, there has been a great deal of support from mental health workers and institutions for the implementation of the Psychiatric Reform. This can be seen in the current technical criteria for a patient to be admitted, which uses multidisciplinary teams, where the subject has the possibility of being fully assessed, minimizing undue admissions and negligence in treatment. Despite this, deconstructing society's idea of madness and offering adequate services to individuals is still a major challenge. The CPRJ seeks to analyze the number of patients who are treated in its emergency department and to find out how many were referred for hospitalization and how many were referred to out-of-hospital services, with the aim of meeting the demands of its territory in the most appropriate way (KAUSEN; CARVALHO, 2008)

CRAZY" DAYS

The observation began in the institution's emergency room, where the reception area was full, which made the researchers uncomfortable because it was a psychiatric emergency room. There was a patient with very altered behaviour, eloquent and disorganized speech. She was clearly in crisis, and remained altered for a long time without being approached by any of the staff, no one went to her side to offer a welcome. When she opened her bag and took out several pills, threatening to take them, she was not noticed by any of the staff. Another patient who was also waiting to be seen, but who was more lucid, called out to the reception staff and showed them what the patient was trying to do with the medication. The employee immediately went to the patient and asked her not to take any medication until she had seen the doctor, asking if she could wait a little longer. The patient said yes and immediately stopped shouting and waited for the doctor to call. It should be remembered that the patient had already caused a stir when she arrived at the unit in the morning, going from the pharmacy to the reception desk shouting that she "needed medicine", going to the counter and reporting in a very aggressive manner to the technician who was there, and who remained calm and seated.

This scene raises the question of the criteria used to organize the care of users, since the nuances in the demand for psychiatric emergency care are notorious, and can vary from the exchange of prescriptions to patients who pose a risk to themselves and others. Behind the reception desk were administrative assistants with an apathetic, defensive posture, who barely looked at those seeking care. They treated all patients in the same way, regardless of whether they had been treated well or not. Even when a more upset patient came up to them in an offensive way, their posture remained the same, rigid but polite, without raising their voices, as if nothing could affect them.

The observations were carried out on different days and at different times of the day, which allowed us to see the dynamics and routine of the CPRJ as a whole. We noticed that in the morning, the emergency room was very busy, but that patients were seen more quickly. In the afternoon, when the flow is much smaller, it was noticed that patients took longer to be seen by the doctors, which meant that the reception desk was constantly full of people waiting. In this way, we questioned whether the fact that patients had to wait for more than an hour was a characteristic of the institution, as this was the minimum time it took for them to be seen every time we were there, regardless of the time and the number of people waiting. An emergency service where patients need to be seen quickly, but end up having to wait for so long, without even being welcomed, denounces a failure to care for them.

During the observations, it was noticed that patients who arrived and went to the counter automatically handed over some form of ID. The administrative technician would check some information and ask the patient to sit down and wait for medical attention without even asking what the demand was. In addition, it was noticed that when an employee called a patient for a consultation, it was done in a low voice, since the emergency room was very large, with several people and external noise, making it difficult to propagate the call. But this wasn't a problem, as the patients sitting there repeated the name of the person being called out loudly, thus helping the staff. Perhaps this was due to the restlessness of waiting to be seen. Patients who arrived confused, looking for information, were promptly helped by other patients who were there waiting for their own appointments. Given that the institution does not provide any staff to perform this function of informing those who arrive.

The dynamics of the institution are mostly carried out by the patients, sometimes leading to an inversion of roles between staff and service users. This can be seen even in the presentation of the technicians, who don't wear any kind of identification badge, making it difficult to differentiate between them and the users.

The situations described above seem to be a characteristic of the emergency service provided in this establishment, often cited by Estellita-Lins (2012) as precarious and disorganized. There is a lack of adequate training and qualification for emergency professionals and a medical system that is systematically geared towards emergency care, leading to a constant blurring of the roles and functions carried out by each professional, highlighting the need for new discussions on the current emergency care model, so that trust can be built between teams, patients and the service, representing and creating new ways of acting in health.

One positive point we noticed in the reception area of the emergency room was that there is a cupboard where books on various subjects are kept, where people can buy them at a low cost or borrow them to read while they are waiting for their appointments. We believe that this is an excellent initiative, especially as the person responsible for looking after the books is a patient, who encourages others to get into the habit of reading. The patients were delighted with the idea and were often seen leafing through the books.

PSYCHIATRIC EMERGENCY

Emergency care is characterized as care that requires immediate medical attention with an imminent risk of death, thus differing from urgent care, which is characterized by not having an immediate risk, but presents a potential risk of aggravation or death, leading to the need for priority care. (MINISTERIO DA SAUDE, 2009)

Currently, 24-hour urgent and emergency care units end up acting as the "gateway" to the public health network, receiving users with urgent conditions, patients who have strayed from the primary care network and social emergencies. These demands are mixed together, overcrowding these establishments and thus compromising the quality of care provided to the population. Psychiatric urgent/emergency care services are particularly concerned with conditions that put the lives of patients and others at risk, such as psychotic or hyperkinetic symptoms, organocerebral decompensation, substance abuse and dependence and the risk of suicide (ORG. LINS, 2012). According to Barros, Tung and Mari (2010), psychiatric emergencies are patients who have disturbances in their thinking, emotions or behavior. As such, they need quick and agile care when they arrive at psychiatric emergency services, so that the doctor can prevent further damage to the individual's psychic, physical and social health.

The above-mentioned authors also discuss issues related to the changes in mental health policy, initiated by the Brazilian health reform, which prioritizes out-of-hospital treatment, giving priority to Primary Health Care. However, the reality of the provision of these services is precarious, leading to greater demand for psychiatric emergencies. It is therefore necessary to manage patients quickly or this will have a direct impact on the functioning of the service, since the demand is disorganized, uninformed and spontaneous. This issue is also linked to the concept of crisis, which, from a biomedical point of view, does not distinguish between the categories of urgency and emergency, giving way to common sense and the autonomy of the reception desks.

Urgent care centers are, in their entirety, environments of great suffering and tension, requiring humanized multi-professional care and qualified listening, welcoming and taking responsibility for the patient from the moment they arrive until they leave the service, expressing an action of bringing the units closer to the patients.

Risk classification is a useful tool that makes it possible to identify the vulnerability and risk of the demand through a careful assessment of the complaint presented and its potential for risk and aggravation. Prioritizing, guiding and deciding on the necessary referrals to solve the user's problem, as well as promptly identifying risk conditions and prioritizing care (MINISTERIO DA SAUDE, 2009).

The dynamics of emergency care at this institution proved to be flawed, with no clear information system for those arriving, no reception criteria or risk classification of users. All that was required was an identification document, from an administrative technician located behind the reception desk, who, after registering, asked them to wait in the waiting room, where the average time could exceed two hours, so that they could be seen by a psychiatrist. There is no kind of reception or responsibility on the part of the unit for those who enter the unit in search of emergency help, going against the humanization guidelines proposed by the Unified Health System.

CONCLUSION

The emergency service observed does not have defined risk criteria, its care is on a first-come, first-served basis with an administrative-bureaucratic reception, which leads to fragmented work with low resolution and overload for the professionals.

Bearing in mind that the psychiatric emergency room is the main service in the mental health network, as it is the gateway to the treatment devices, as well as providing assistance to excess demand, it is believed that the technical team should value listening to demand, as this could be an effective way of changing the configuration of care and providing more qualified assistance, encouraging interdisciplinary work and integrated action with the mental health network.

REFERENCES

BARROS, S.; SALLES, MARIANA. Management of mental health care in the Unified Health System. **Rev. Esc. Enferm.** *USP*, Sao Paulo, v. 45, n. Esp. 2, p. 1780-1785, 2011.

BARROS, R. E. M.; TENG, C. T.; MARI, J. J. Psychiatric emergency services and their relationship with the Brazilian mental health network. **Revista Brasileira de Psiquiatria**, v. 32, supl. II, p. 71-77, 2010.

BRAZIL. Ministry of Health. Law n.8.080, of September 19, 1990. Diario Oficial da Uniao, Brasilia, September 20, 1990. Section 1.

BRAZIL. Ministry of Health. Law n. 10.216 of April 6, 2001, on mental health, protection and rights of people with mental disorders and redirects the care model. Official Gazette of the Federative Republic of Brazil. Brasilia, April 6, 2001.

BRAZIL. Ministry of Health. Health Care Secretariat. National Policy for the Humanization of SUS Care and Management. Reception and risk classification in emergency services / Ministerio da Saude, Secretaria de Atengao a Saude, Polltica Nacional de Humanizagao da Atengao e Gestao do SUS. - Brasilia, 2009. 56 p.: ill. color. - (Serie B. Textos Basicos de Saude)

BEZERRA JR, B. Desafios da Reforma Psiquiatrica no Brasil. **Physis: Rev. Saude Coletiva**, Rio de Janeiro, v. 17, n. 2, p. 243-250, 2007.

DEL-BEN, C. M.; TENG, C. T. Emergência psiquiatrica: desafios e vicissitudes, **Revista Brasileira de Psiquiatria**, Sao Paulo, v. 32, supl II, p. 67-68, Oct. 2010.

DELGADO, P. G. G. Democracy and psychiatric reform in Brazil. **Ciencia & Saude Coletiva**, v. 16, n. 12, p. 4701-4706, 2011.

ESTELLITA-LINS, C. (Org.). **Trading six for half a dozen**: Suicide as an emergency in Rio de Janeiro. Rio de Janeiro: Mauad, 2012, 160 p.

KEUSEN, A.; CARVALHO, A. L. The construction of a territorially based service: the experience of the Psychiatric Center of Rio de Janeiro. **Saude em Debate**, Rio de Janeiro, v. 32, n. 78/79/80, p. 161-171, 2008.

PAULIN, L. F.; TURATO, E. R. Background to psychiatric reform in Brazil: the contradictions of the 1970s. **Historia, Ciencia, Saude**, Manguinhos, v. 11, n. 2, p. 241258, 2004.

PRANDONIL, R. F. S.; PADILHA, M. I. C. S. **Texto Contexto Enferm.**, v. 13, n. 4, p. 633-640, 2004.

Chapter 2

RIO DE JANEIRO PSYCHIATRIC CENTER: PSYCHIATRIC REFORM IN THE GAMBOA REGION

Cristiane de Carvalho Guimaraes

Rosane da Costa Albuquerque Erika Barbosa de Araujo

INTRODUCTION

This article aims to present the Rio de Janeiro Psychiatric Center (CPRJ) as a small mental health care network in the city of Rio de Janeiro. It also presents the beginnings of its implementation and the history of the Gamboa region, a region that has relevant historical landmarks. Bibliographic and documentary research were used as sources for gathering data. Texts with historical information about the city of Rio de Janeiro and the Gamboa region were analyzed, as well as the history and analysis of the Brazilian Psychiatric Reform and the federal legislation that underpins this process.

The results point to a service that plays a fundamental role in the community where it is located and projects in line with the perspectives of the Brazilian Psychiatric Reform. It is a service that deserves in-depth study, given its peculiarities, especially its living spaces, where we learn to deal with madness.

2 THE BEGINNING OF THE STORY

Gamboa's history is intertwined with the expansion of Rio de Janeiro's city center and the slave trade. Slavery left a deep mark on the city and especially on this neighborhood. Its history dates back to the 16th century, when the sea still reached the region of Gamboa and Saude. According to Coaracy (2009), the discovery of gold and diamonds in Minas Gerais led to an immediate need for slaves, which turned the port of Rio de Janeiro into an important trading post. The main place for disembarking and trading blacks was in what is now Praqa Quinze. The movement caused by the growth in the arrival of slave ships and the presence of captives around the square bothered the Portuguese court which, in a press campaign, pressured the Marquis of Lavradio to remove the market. Around 1770, the Marquis decided to move the slave market to the Valongo area, which at the time was occupied by farms, vegetable gardens and small animal husbandry. The move, according to Coaracy (2009), caused significant changes in the region's economy. Markets, trapiches (warehouses for imported goods, including slaves) and manufactories (handicrafts) were set up. Areas were plotted, increasing the supply of land for new buildings, the marshes were landfilled and, in a short time, the region grew and developed.

According to Coaracy (2009), when traveling on slave ships, many slaves died and their bodies were thrown overboard. Others died shortly after disembarking and were buried in churchyards or simply abandoned on the beaches and in the streets. Recently, many bones have been found in this region and have given rise to a museum (MEMORIAL DOS PRETOS NOVOS, 2016). Those who survived were fed, clothed and, having recovered from their hard journey, sold at the Valongo market, which was close to what is now Rua Sacadura Cabral. Coaracy (2009) tells us that, on the days of their departure for forced labor in the mines and on the plantations, the blacks would drum and sing to kill some of the nostalgia for their land.

In 1843, Empress Tereza Cristina arrived in Brazil, at which time the Valongo pier was renovated and renamed Cais da Imperatriz. Rua do Valongo was renamed Rua da Imperatriz and remained so until 1890, when it was renamed after a Paraguayan war hero, Francisco Camerino de Azevedo.

Between the end of the 18th century and the beginning of the 19th century, Gamboa was a very picturesque neighborhood, chosen by the aristocracy and wealthy families as the location for their chacaras and palaces.

From the end of the 19th century, Gamboa lost its status, as the aristocracy moved to the neighborhoods of Catete, Gloria, Flamengo, Botafogo and Laranjeiras, fleeing the proximity to the port.

At the end of the 19th century and the beginning of the 20th century, the term "favela" appeared in Gamboa, since a large number of soldiers who took part in the Canudos War[1] , many of them from the North and Northeast, built precarious dwellings there, as they didn't have decent accommodation. Favela was a reference to a place bordering the Canudos arraial in Bahia where the troops probably stayed or where the fighting took place. These precarious housing solutions were located on the slopes of Morro da Providencia.

The first samba circles were also born in this region. The drums played in the hills and in the plagues, translating the pain and suffering of existence into music. Popular culture has a strong presence there, including characters and entities linked to the Rio Carnival. Donga and Joao da Baiana, great names in samba, held lively samba circles on the steps of Pedra do Sal, near Praga Maua. This was a mandatory route for those heading to Tia Ciata's house in Praga Onze.

[1] The so-called Canudos War, Canudos Revolution or Canudos Insurrection, was a confrontation between a popular socio-religious movement and the Army of the Republic, which lasted from 1896 to 1897, in the then community of Canudos, in the interior of the state of Bahia, Brazil. (SOUZA, 2016)

It's important to note that, after work began on Porto Maravilha[2] , archaeological studies and excavations began in the region and rescued its historical and cultural importance for understanding the process of African Diaspora[3] and the formation of Brazilian society. In the mid-19th century, the region was known as "Little Africa", as it contained the largest concentration of Africans outside Africa.

Motivated by these findings, the city government then created Municipal Decree No. 34.803, of November 29, 2011 (RIO DE JANEIRO, 2011), the Curatorial Working Group of the Historical and Archaeological Circuit of African Heritage, in order to collectively build guidelines for implementing policies to enhance the memory and protection of this cultural heritage.

In the middle of the 20th century, the first center for the treatment of people with mental disorders appeared in this territory marked by blood, sweat and tears - the CPRJ - Centro Psiquiatrico Rio de Janeiro.

3 THE TERRITORY OF MADNESS

The current CPRJ was born out of the desire of its patients, families and technicians, who had previously been working in Rua Venezuela, in a place called PAM da Venezuela. In the 1970s and 1980s, this PAM (Posto de Atendimento Medico) had been the general center for psychiatric admissions, the top billing place for hospital admission authorizations (AIH)[4] in Rio de Janeiro.

This unit was deactivated due to the repossession of the property by the Federal Ministry of Justice, leaving the mental health service homeless. In a joint effort that brought together all the interested parties (patients, family members and technicians), the search began for a site near the old building that could house the service. After much searching, one of the patients discovered that in Praga da Harmonia there was an abandoned building that had been used as a shelter for the indigent. After negotiations, discussions and many difficulties, the CPRJ was allowed to move to its new address. The building, although very beautiful and well-structured, was not in good condition. Everyone had to pull together to make the building habitable. The CPRJ then began its activities in August 1998, occupying a

---

[2] Porto Maravilha is a revitalization program of the Rio de Janeiro City Hall, with the support of the State Government and the Ministry of Tourism, which aims to requalify the city's "Port Region" (Caju, Gamboa, Saude and Santo Cristo), which has suffered great degradation due to the lack of incentives for industry and housing since the 60s. The project envisages the development of the region based on the principles of sustainability, with the restructuring of streets, squares and avenues, improving the quality of life of the current and future inhabitants of the Gamboa hill. The urban operation covers an area of 5 million square meters[2] , whose boundaries are Presidente Vargas, Rodrigues Alves, Rio Branco and Francisco Bicalho Avenues. (RIO DE JANEIRO, 2016)

[3] African Diaspora is the socio-cultural and historical phenomenon that took place in African countries due to the forced immigration of the African population to countries that were characterized by the existence of slave labor. This happened at the beginning of the Modern Age and lasted until the end of the 18th century (FLORENTINO, 2009).

[4] Hospital units participating in the SUS send information on hospitalizations to municipal or state managers, containing data on hospitalizations in Brazil (DATASUS, 2016).

building located at Praga Coronel Assungao s/n°, Praga da Harmonia.

The implementation of the service was facilitated by the time it took place, given the guiding principles of the Unified Health System (SUS), such as universality, equity and comprehensiveness. The assumptions of the Italian Psychiatric Reform were therefore well known, and the Brazilian Psychiatric Reform was already underway, highlighting the ineffectiveness of the asylum model that had predominated until the end of the first half of the 20th century. There were also the first community centers and substitute services (Psychosocial Care Centers - CAPS, Day Hospitals, among others).

The Brazilian Psychiatric Reform Movement has as its hallmark the struggle to overcome the asylum, the defense of the extension of citizenship rights to people with mental disorders and the call for society to build a "new social place for madness". Mental Health in Brazil has therefore been restructured in order to meet the demands of individuals with such disorders.

This process of restructuring encourages reflection and practical initiatives in various fields. And the construction of this new place for the insane is intrinsically placed in the meanders of these fields. But how do we build this new place?

Saraceno (2001, p.16) points out that this process involves a "[...] reconstruction, a full exercise of citizenship, and also of full contractuality in the three major scenarios: habitat, social network and work with social value".

In this sense, pioneering work helps to understand the complexity of the issue. The team at the Prof. Luiz da Rocha Cerqueira Psychosocial Care Center in Sao Paulo - which has been working on this issue for 20 years - believes that this reconstruction can only be achieved through the work of the center. Luiz da Rocha Cerqueira Psychosocial Care Center in Sao Paulo - whose work has been going on for more than 20 years -, for example, understands that this reconstruction can only be consolidated when the person establishes a more autonomous life, managing their affective and professional relationships and the territory, understood as the inhabited geographical space, instituted of meanings and affections, spaces of social lakes and guarantees of quality of life, a relational reality, made up, on the one hand, of natural, geographical objects, and, on the other, of society in movement (LEITAO; BARROS, 2012).

4 CPRJ'S MADNESS TODAY

The CPRJ, as an agency of the Rio de Janeiro State Department of Health and Civil

Defense (SESDEC), belongs to the group of emergency hospitals. Although it belongs to this state department, it works within the psychosocial care network of the municipality of Rio de Janeiro, with the aim of better serving the flow of people with mental disorders who need treatment. It is currently the only psychiatric emergency room in operation in the state.

It has an open-door emergency service that does not only serve patients living in the area, but also has an important influx of residents from other areas of the city and a small participation from some municipalities. It offers short-stay hospitalization, around six days, and outpatient and day hospital care, with psychosocial support and health promotion actions.

It is also a training ground, hosting multi-professional residents from Rio de Janeiro State University (UERJ).

According to information from the then Coordinator of Psychosocial Actions[5] (GUIMARAES, 2014), the CPRJ has four integrated care sectors operating in the same two-storey building:

1st Entrance Door consists of a reception with three administrative staff responsible for filling in the entry form, searching for medical records and so on; a table with chairs for checking vital signs by the nursing staff; four consulting rooms for medical and psychological care; three rooms for social services; a nursing station that also supports the outpatient clinic; a short-stay bed for observation and an Ombudsman's office.

2nd Outpatient Clinic - has a reception with three administrative staff; ten consulting rooms for medical and psychological care; a consulting room for social care and a nursing station, which also serves the front door. It is open from Monday to Friday from 8am to 5pm and on Saturdays from 8am to 1pm, with the support of the pharmacy which dispenses the medication, or part of it, needed to continue treatment. The CPRJ outpatient clinic also runs a project aimed at the elderly population, Pater, (Projeto de Atenqao a Terceira Idade), which carries out neuropsychological assessments of patients with suspected dementia and Alzheimer's disease .[6]

3rd Emergency Ward - offers twenty beds distributed over three wards, eight places for men and twelve for women; an internal courtyard for activities, an Occupational Therapy room and a multidisciplinary assessment room. Most of the admissions come from the front

---

[5] Interview given to the authors as part of the research project "The voice of mental health users", by Cristiane Guimaraes (2014), in February/15.

[6] Alzheimer's is an incurable disease that worsens over time, but it can and must be treated. Almost all of its victims are elderly people. Perhaps this is why the disease has become wrongly known as "sclerosis" or "lapsing". The disease presents as dementia, or loss of cognitive functions (memory, orientation, attention and language), caused by the death of brain cells. When diagnosed at an early stage, it is possible to delay its progression and have more control over the symptoms, ensuring a better quality of life for the patient and their family. (ABRAz - Associapao Brasileira de Alzheimer, 2016)

door.

4° Centro de Convivencia e Hospital-Dia - occupies the second floor of the building and has a reception with three administrative staff; a reception and group room; a nursing room; a kitchen; a laundry room; a library; a theater; yarn workshop (sewing); painting and canvas workshop; a room for the association of relatives and users (AFAUCEP)[7] ; a workshop for recovering furniture (patina and others); an art gallery; a room for storing thrift store material and a room for music therapy.

The Day-Hospital has around 140 registered users, says the CPRJ Psychosocial Actions Coordinator, with varying therapeutic contracts, who can attend the number of days a week that best suits their needs and possibilities. This clientele includes people from the project to assist the homeless population with mental disorders.

In addition to the specific service sectors, the CPRJ has a cafeteria for patients and professionals; an auditorium; a canteen; two administrative rooms (general and technical management); a scientific documentation sector; a human resources room; a pharmacy; an administrative management room and one for the storeroom.All the service sectors have male and female toilets. There is an internal patio next to the outpatient waiting corridor where therapeutic activities are also carried out. The CPRJ also has three vehicles, one ambulance and two vehicles for administrative support, home visits and others.

The day hospital that serves users believes in creativity and uses art as therapy. Painting, music, theater or even cooking are some of the activities worked on in the therapeutic workshops, which function as a living center, where the user spends the day participating in playful activities, experiencing a sensory universe, in which new possibilities of existence are appearing. Breaking away from the exclusion and prejudices surrounding those who are considered insane is one of the great challenges facing the Day Hospital team who, despite working with sometimes demanding resources, believe in their work. As Keuzen and Carvalho (2008) tell us,

> [...] the whole process of building the diversity of activities was only possible because of the commitment of technicians, users and their families who, through public debates, assemblies and team meetings, tried to find solutions to improve the assistance provided by the CPRJ.

The environment of the Day Hospital, with its wide, bright corridors, designed by the modernist architect Reidy[8] , arouses the curiosity of visitors. The space, which houses

[7] Association of relatives and users of the Psychiatric Center

[8] Affonso Eduardo Reidy (Paris, 26/10/1909 - Rio de Janeiro, 10/08/1964) was a Brazilian architect. He is considered one of the

exhibitions of paintings, collages and sculptures produced by the patients, is pleasant, airy and full of color. The room where the cooking workshops take place is spacious and organized. The small theater has a closet full of costumes for different types of shows. There is also the workshop where the allegories for the "Tremendo nos Nervos" carnival block are produced. One of the very special fruits of the team's work is the musical group Harmonia Enlouquece, which has long since surpassed the white door of the Hospital (which is always open) and has even performed at the Canecao concert hall, among other places in Rio de Janeiro. The musical group was created by psychologist and music therapist Sidnei M. Dantas, as part of the "Convivendo com a Musica" (Living with Music) project, and gives voice to the "musical deliriums" of patients, hospital staff and other partners who find a way of expressing themselves in music.

A visit to the Day Hospital can be translated as a rich experience through the universe of play, the sensation of being inside one of Frederico Fellini's films[9] in which madness coexists so well with art.

The CPRJ aims to work in an integrated way with its surroundings. Its history and work, as well as its interaction with the health care network, are little known, although it is understood that this inclusion in the community is fundamental, that is, the fact that it is part of the territory, so that the exclusion experienced by users in the past is not established.

One of the hallmarks of the substitution service model, according to Onocko- Campos and Furtado (2006), is the need to work in the territory, which goes beyond the geographical space, crossing subjectivity and the subject's immersion. But, after all, how does one define whether or not the service works in the territory? At first, it is understood that it is not enough for the service to be geographically located in a certain place. The construction of the notion of territory effectively involves the service taking root in the community, establishing social ties and bonds, and engaging in dialogue with the organizations around it: residents' associations, churches, security services, fire departments, clubs, carnival blocks and businesses. In short, in the places where life happens. In order to do this, the service needs to be open to building this territory.

Since its creation, the CPRJ has maintained close ties with the community. Today, it is the headquarters of the Municipal Security Council and actively participates in the neighborhood's political movement. Its users are part of the neighborhood's cultural

pioneers in the introduction of modern architecture in the country, and is one of the great names of modern urbanism in the country (BRUAND, 2002).

[9] Federico Fellini (Rimini, 20/01/1920 Rome, 31/10/1993) was one of the most important Italian filmmakers. He became famous for the poetry of his films, which, even when they made serious criticisms of society, preserved the magic of cinema. (UNIVERSO ON LINE, 2016)

movements, such as the Prata Preta and Cia de Misterios carnival blocks. Users also take part in cultural meetings at the Memorial dos Pretos Novos, which is part of the Instituto de Pesquisa e Memoria Pretos Novos - IPN (Institute for Research and Memory of the Pretos Novos), which aims to reflect on slavery in Brazil and develop educational and research projects to preserve the memory of the Pretos Novos. The CPRJ is also one of the venues of the "Clube da Esquina"[10] , welcoming users and their families for weekend activities.

Much has been said and proposed, in terms of legislation and practice, about integrating mental health services into the community. As we can see in the 2007-2010 Management Report (BRASIL, 2011, p.29):

> From 2003 to 2010, this restructuring of psychiatric hospital care took place in a coordinated and agreed process, which allowed the reduction in the number of beds and psychiatric hospitals to be concatenated with the construction and progressive expansion of an open, diversified and community-integrated care network, strategically based on Psychosocial Care Centers (CAPS), mental health centers in basic care, the Back to Home Program and social inclusion programs through work.

Community integration and interaction is not an easy practice to implement. The same 2007-2010 Management Report (BRASIL, 2011, p.40) states that:

> General Hospitals, because they work according to the logic of clinical specialties, present many barriers to the interface with the community and the articulation with the mental health network and the territories. The field of mental health has also historically been very distant from discussions about the organization of care in General Hospitals.

It's been many years of a possibly troubled relationship, given the relationship of exclusion and fear experienced by both sides: people with mental disorders and communities. The so-called "normal" community, afraid of the so-called "freaks" who would be violent and unstable; the so-called "freaks", afraid of being rejected and sent back to large hospital institutions, from where they often took years to leave. This is what Oliveira et al (2012) say:

> Users report that they still suffer a lot of prejudice, are stigmatized by their families, neighbors, the community in general and by some

[10] Clube da Esquina, a project created at the Institute of Psychiatry of the Federal University of Rio de Janeiro, in partnership with other psychiatric services, is a multi-professional Saturday leisure project that now covers the greater Rio area (MIRANDA, 2011).

> professionals who work in health, whether in other care networks, in CAPS itself or in public service networks in general [...]

5 IS THERE SPACE FOR THE CPRJ IN PSYCHOSOCIAL CARE HISTORY?

Rio de Janeiro, like other Brazilian cities and states, has been undergoing a reorganization of its health services as part of the struggle for a more democratic country and health system.

This reorganization has as an important goal the administrative and financial decentralization of health in the country, i.e. the implementation of municipal and state autonomy in the management of financial and material resources in the area of health.

> Considering these assumptions, various movements were made, both in conferences and in other forums, involving technicians, users and professionals, seeking to comply with the principles of the SUS. In the municipalities, there were changes to achieve a new organization of health services, mainly from the point of view of building care models that were appropriate to the respective local and regional realities. The actors in this decentralization process, public and private service providers, health professionals and users of the system, have both the autonomy to develop programs and strategies more suited to their reality and the responsibility to conduct and implement health policies and actions, in accordance with the demands and potential identified (KLEBA, 2005 apud BASTOS, 2012).

Within this process, mental health is experiencing the proposal of deinstitutionalization, which, in the context of the Reform, has a greater ethical dimension. It means much more than reorganizing care for the so-called insane. It's not just about overcoming the asylum, but about building a new way for society to deal with madness.

With the passing of Federal Law 10.216/2001[11] , the time has come to replace the old asylum paradigm with a new, community-based paradigm, integrated into society and the general health system.

The Brazilian Psychiatric Reform is an ongoing process that has many facets. According to Pitta (2011, p.4580), there is already evidence in the country of greater levels of individual and social effectiveness for people with mental disorders who are being treated in the community, when compared to those treated in prison.

Since the CPRJ was set up in 1998, its fundamental task has been to provide mental

[11] Law No. 10.216, of April 6, 2001. Provides for the protection and rights of people with mental disorders and redirects the mental health care model (BRASIL, 2001).

health care. Even outside the structure provided for in the new political proposals[12] , the CPRJ has been providing care to the entire program area[13] in the region covering the city center to Gloria, from Sao Cristovao to Mare. There have been many comings and goings over this period. Today, however, the question is: is there still room for a service with these characteristics?

In its operating model, one objective is central: to coordinate the link between crisis care and the assistance necessary for the process of re-socialization of the population served, in an agile manner, with humanized care, resolutive and integrated into the mental health care network.

The CPRJ, however, is not a Caps, where psychosocial care prevails and not just medication.

> [...] CAPS are strategic services for organizing the mental health care network and consolidating the Brazilian Psychiatric Reform. Their operation follows the guidelines issued by the Ministry of Health, which differentiate the services according to the population density of the territory or municipality, opening hours, population served, crisis reception capacity, as well as the professionals who make up the team. CAPS have the organizational configuration of CAPS I, CAPS II and CAPS III, depending on the complexity of the services and the population's responsibility. CAPS I would have the operational capacity to serve municipalities with a population of over 20,000 people, and CAPS II, to serve municipalities with a population of over 70,000 people. CAPS III and CAPS III AD (alcohol and drugs) would have the capacity to serve municipalities with populations of over 200,000 inhabitants, with the difference compared to the previous ones of being a 24-hour continuous care service, including holidays and weekends, and having beds integrated into the service for night-time reception. (FAGUNDES JUNIOR et al, 2016)

It can be said that the way the CPRJ works is similar to a Caps III, as Keuzen and Carvalho (2008) have already said:

> This presentation of an experience at the CPRJ highlights that its

[12] The IV National Conference on Mental Health - Intersectoral (CNSM-I) reaffirms the Psychosocial Care Center - CAPS - as a fundamental device in the psychosocial care model that replaces psychiatric hospitals, highlighting its strategic role as an articulator of the network of services and the need to strengthen intersectoral partnerships and intensify communication between CAPS, the mental health network and the general health network, taking into account the intra- and intersectoral dimensions. Final Report of the IV National Conference on Mental Health - Intersectoral, June 27 to July 1, 2010. Brasilia: National Health Council/Ministry of Health, 2010, p.210 (BRASIL, 2010)

[13] The city of Rio de Janeiro is divided into 10 Program Areas. Rio de Janeiro has an area of 1,224 km2 and a population density of 5,163 inhabitants/Km2. It is organized into 33 Administrative Regions (AR) and 160 neighbourhoods. The city is very heterogeneous, with varying degrees of development and, consequently, inequality in the distribution and use of available resources, including health services. For health planning purposes, the municipality is part of the Metropolitan Health Region I of the state of Rio de Janeiro. To the same end, the Municipal Health Department has been working since 1993 to divide the city into 10 Planning Areas (AP) (RIO DE JANEIRO, 2011).

> current care model is closer to the functions of a Caps type III (Brazil, 2004), i.e. a mental health unit aimed at people with severe and persistent mental disorders who have difficulty establishing social bonds. The major difference is that the CPRJ still has a psychiatric emergency room and still fulfills the function of evaluating psychiatric hospitalization for the city of Rio de Janeiro.

It is, however, a service of the state of Rio de Janeiro, not of the municipality, like most of the 29 Caps in the city, according to Fagundes Junior et al (2016). And its possible transformation into a Caps would not be a simple task, as it is an integrated service, with all the care modalities. It is, in itself, a "small" mental health network. It therefore works differently. If in the day hospital the logic is that of psychosocial care, in the crisis ward, the emergency room and the outpatient clinic, the logic is that of medication. These ways of approaching care create a tension, a struggle between the different models, which build up a specific form of the institution. Different professionals, with different technical, ethical and personal understandings, help to confront the models that coexist on a daily basis. Possibly what ensures that an institution remains alive and productive is precisely the possibility of questioning and confrontation. Conflicts are healthy and absolutely pedagogical. Users perceive the differences in care models and join one or the other, discussing whether what prevails is the logic of medication. They live with different forms of care and realize that the richness is not the predominance of one or the other, but, above all, the conflict brought to the center of the debate.

It is understood that the model of institutionalization (keeping users in the service for long periods) only ends when the debate, discussion and conflicts that arise in the day-to-day running of the institution can be exposed, brought to light.

> This allows us to demarcate the possibility of developing services in large cities that can act in an integral way and be integrated into the network, providing territorial care for clients, whether in crisis, in their daily demands or in the rehabilitation process. (KEUZEN; CARVALHO, 2008, p.170)

There is no ideal service, totally integrated into the community, resolute in every way. There are, as in the CPRJ, spaces of coexistence, where we come to understand that we need to learn more and more to deal with madness.

REFERENCES

ABRAZ. Brazilian Alzheimer's Association. Available at: <http://abraz.org.br/sobre-alzheimer/o-que-e-alzheimer>. Accessed on: October 7, 2016.

BASTOS, F. R. A. **The decentralization process in the unified health system in Brazil.** XVII Congreso Internacional del CLAD sobre la Reforma del Estado y de la Administracion Publica, Cartagena, Colombia, 30 oct. - 2 Nov. 2012 Documento Libre.

UNI VERSOONLINE. **Federico Felini**. Available at: <http://educacao.uol.com.br/biografias/federico-fellini.htm.> Accessed on: October 7, 2016.

BRAZIL. Federal Law 10.216/2001. **Provides for the protection and rights of people with mental disorders and redirects the mental health care model.** Presidency of the Republic Casa Civil, Subchefia para Assuntos Juridicos, Brasilia, DF, April 6, 2001.

BRAZIL. Ministry of Health. **Management Report** (2007-2010). The New Frontiers of Psychiatric Reform, 2011.

BRAZIL. Ministry of Health. **Final Report of the IV National Conference on Mental Health** - Intersectoral, June 27 to July 1, 2010. Brasilia: National Health Council/Ministry of Health, 2010, p.210.

BRAZIL. Ministry of Health. **Datasus**. SUS Information Department. Available at: <http://datasus.saude.gov.br/tabelas-do-aih>. Accessed on October 7, 2016.

BRUAND, Y. **Contemporary architecture in Brazil.** Sao Paulo: Perspectiva Publishing House, 2002.

COARACY, V. **O Rio de Janeiro do Seculo XVII.** Rio de Janeiro, 2009.

FAGUNDES JUNIOR, H. M.; DESVIAT, M.; SILVA, P. R. F. Psychiatric reform in Rio de Janeiro: current situation and future prospects. **Ciencia & Saude Coletiva**, 21(5): 1449-1460, 2016. Available at: <http://www.scielo.br/scielo.php?pid=S141381232016000501449&script=sci_abstract&tlng=en.> Accessed on: October 08, 2016.

FLORENTINO, M. The African diaspora**. Duetto Magazine**. Living History. Available at: <http://www2.uol.com.br/historiaviva/reportagens/ a_diaspora_africana_imprimir.html.> Accessed on October 7, 2016.

GUIMARAES, C. C. **The voice of Mental Health users:** a study at the Day Hospital of the

Rio de Janeiro Psychiatric Center. Rio de Janeiro: Estacio de Sa University, 2014.

KEUSEN, A.; CARVALHO, A. A construção de um serviço de base territorial: a experiência do Centro Psiquiatrico rio de Janeiro. **Revista Saude em Debate,** vol.32, n.78/79/80, Jan/Dec 2008.

KLEBA, M.E. **Decentralization of the health system in Brazil**: limits and possibilities of a strategy for empowerment. Chapeco: Argos, 2005.

LEITAO, A. e BARROS, S. Territorio e Serviqo Comunitario de Saude Mental: as concepqões presentes nos discursos dos atores do processo da reforma psiquiatrica brasileira. **Saude Soc. Sao Paulo, v.21, n.3, p.572-586, 2012**. Available at < http://www.scielo.br/pdf/sausoc/v21n3/05.pdf >. Accessed on: October 12, 2016.

MEMORIAL OF THE NEW BLACKS. Available at: <http://www.museusdorio.com.br/joomla/index.php?option=com_k2&view=item&id=83: memorial-dos-pretos-novos> Accessed on 15/10/2016

MIRANDA, C.M.L. O cuidado como inclusao do sujeito. **Anna Nery School. Journal of Nursing.** Rio de Janeiro: UFRJ, 2011.

OLIVEIRA, R. F.; ANDRADE, L. O. M.; GOYA, N. Access and comprehensiveness: the understanding of users of a mental health network. **Ciencia e Saude Coletiva.** 17(11): 3069-3078, 2012.

ONOCKO-CAMPOS, R.; FURTADO, J. P. Between collective health and mental health: a methodological tool for evaluating the network of psychosocial care centers (CAPS) of the Unified Health System. **Cad. Saude Publica**, v.22, n.5, p. 1053-62, 2006. Available at: <http://www.scielo.br/scielo.php?script=sci_arttext&pid=S0102-311X2006000500018> Accessed on: March 07, 2016.

PITTA, A. M. F. A review of the Brazilian psychiatric reform: institutions, actors and policies. **Cienc. saude coletiva,** Rio de Janeiro , v. 16, n. 12, p. 4579-4589, Dec. 2011 Available at: <http://www.scielo.br/scielo.php?script=sci_arttext&pid=S1413 81232011001300002&lng=en&nrm=iso>. Accessed on: October 10, 2016.

RIO DE JANEIRO (City). **Porto Maravilha**. Available at: <http://www.portomaravilha.com.br/.> Accessed on October 7, 2016.

RIO DE JANEIRO (City). Municipal Decree No. 34.803, of November 29, 2011. **Creates the Historical and Archaeological Circuit for the Celebration of African Heritage and**

the Curatorial Working Group for the circuit's Urban, Architectural and Museological Project, 2011. Available at: <http://www.portomaravilha.com.br/conteudo/legislacao/decretos/d34803.pdf.> Accessed on 10/10/2016.

RIO DE JANEIRO (City). **Rio de Janeiro Municipal Health Plan**. PMS 2014 - 2017 Municipal Health Secretariat. Rio de Janeiro, 2013. Available at < http://www.rio.rj.gov.br/dlstatic/10112/3700816/4128745/PMS_20142017.pdf.> Accessed on: October 07, 2016.

SARACENO, B. **Liberating Identities -** From Social Rehabilitation to Possible Citizenship. 2. ed. Rio de Janeiro: Te Cora/Instituto Franco Basaglia, 2001.

SOUSA, R. G. **Guerra de Canudos**. Brazil School. Available at <http://brasilescola.uol.com.br/historiab/canudos.htm.> Accessed on October 07, 2016.

Chapter 3

THE VOICE OF USERS

Cristiane de Carvalho Guimaraes Erika Barbosa de Araujo

INTRODUCTION

The research 'The voice of mental health users: a study at the day hospital of the Rio de Janeiro Psychiatric Center' began in February 2015 and aimed to investigate the social representation of users of a mental health service about the changes that the Brazilian Psychiatric Reform proposes to make. The service chosen was the Rio de Janeiro Psychiatric Center (CPRJ), located in Gamboa, downtown Rio de Janeiro. The CPRJ is an integrated mental health care center under the administration of the Rio de Janeiro State Health Department (SES/RJ) that was created in August 1998. The CPRJ offers various types of treatment today: Day Hospital (HD); 24-hour Emergency Care; Crisis Ward; Outpatient Clinic.

The sample consisted of a group of twenty users who had previously been hospitalized for at least three months (uninterrupted or not) and who had now been attending the mental health facility's day hospital for at least the same period. The three-month period was considered sufficient for the subject to experience being a user of an institution and therefore be considered a representative individual of these two realities. The users were not chosen according to their pathology.

The CPRJ is located in an area with abundant road traffic. This factor contributes to the region having a larger floating, non-resident population than the local resident population (a factor that cannot be ignored, since the CPRJ serves the population under its jurisdiction, being an emergency unit and one of the gateways to the mental health care network). The representative population therefore included individuals from other regions, with a history of hospitalizations and experiences in mental health facilities.

It is worth noting that in the state of Rio de Janeiro, the CPRJ day hospital is one of the last in operation (apart from the CPRJ day hospital, there is only the day hospital at the Psychiatry Institute of the University of Brazil, UFRJ). This type of care, as stated in the 2003-2006 SUS Management Report, despite its historical importance in changing the mental health care model, has been updated in light of the role played by the Psychosocial Care Centers.

Despite being considered by this same report as a service in the process of being overtaken and belonging to the State Health Department, HD works as part of the psychosocial care network of the municipality of Rio de Janeiro, aiming to improve the flow of people with mental disorders who need treatment.

It's also important to note that HD operates within a system - the CPRJ - which is an integrated service, with all the modalities of care. It is, in itself, a "small" mental health network. It therefore operates differently. Certainly, this peculiar way of working also leads to the establishment of peculiar relationships. It is common for users, when in crisis, to be admitted to the service itself; or for them to be, at the same time, users of the HD and the outpatient clinic, for example. This was taken into account when analyzing the speeches collected.

The research was supported by the Research Productivity Program of the Estacio de Sa University and the ethical and scientific norms for conducting research with human beings were observed in accordance with Resolution 196 of October 10, 1996 of the National Health Council, and the project was approved by the Research Ethics Committee of the same University.

1 - THE FIRST CONTACTS

The first contact with the CPRJ was made via e-mail with its Director, who forwarded the research summary to the Institution's Ethics Committee, which approved it. The research had already been approved by Plataforma Brasil (Opinion Number: 727.015).

During their first visits to the CPRJ, the researchers took part in some of the activities developed by the users and technicians, such as the therapeutic cooking workshop, the music workshop and the reception. At all times, the researchers were introduced to the users and they were totally willing to tell their stories in the interviews. It's important to note that these visits were important for the researchers to get to know the users and the technical team, clearing up any doubts that might interfere with the aim of the research and the possible use of the data collected.

Particularly noteworthy was the participation and presentation of the research at the User Assembly. From then on, the interviews with users were scheduled.

2 - DESCRIBING USERS

A total of 22 users were interviewed, 7 women and 15 men, ranging in age from 28 to 65 (two interviews were discarded from the analysis because the users didn't fit the defined criteria perfectly. Naturally, the researchers only found out when the interview was in progress and it was not possible - nor would it have been polite - to interrupt it).

The interviews took place inside the CPRJ in rooms that were available and had privacy. The times were set according to the users' availability, always in the afternoon. All of the users had been hospitalized several times, some of them for very long periods of up to a year. It was not possible to specify the number and length of each hospitalization. The interviewees don't know exactly this information and collecting this data would require visits to several institutions, so through information in medical records, a parameter of stays was obtained.

Their levels of education range from incomplete primary education to complete higher education. Of those interviewed, six did not report any occupation and/or profession. Eight of them are retired, five do not receive any benefits and/or pensions and the others receive the Continuous Cash Benefit from the Social Assistance Organic Law (BPC/Loas). Their pathologies are not clearly defined, either by them or by their medical records, through the ICD (International Classification of Diseases), ranging from paranoid schizophrenia, unspecified schizophrenia, severe depressive episode with psychotic symptoms and severe depression, to "nerve problems". In terms of nosographic classification, using an expression from classical psychiatry, it can be said that their diagnoses are not a central concern of the institution's mental health team. The HD doesn't work under the domination of the medical reference as happens (or used to happen) in many psychiatric institutions. There is a psychiatric assessment, medical and pharmacological follow-up by the team's psychiatrists, but there is no major concern on the part of the team to establish an ICD.

Twelve users have a support network based on their family, mother, siblings and partner. Seven of them have no family or social support and one of them has a friend who manages his benefit and lives with him. Two live in public shelters

One user has been attending the CPRJ day hospital since its creation 16 years ago. Others have been attending for between 3 and 15 years. In other words, an average of 8 years as users of the service.

They all take part in activities at the HD. These are the workshops that make up the therapeutic project developed for each user, consisting of the period of stay, which varies between 3 and 5 days a week at the HD, and participation in the workshops, according to the profile of each one. This therapeutic project aims to develop skills and restore citizenship. The workshops involve cooking, music, painting and making carnival costumes, for example. There are also therapeutic groups run by the technical team.

Users take part in meetings called assemblies with the technical team, where they present news about their particular demands, such as medical care for those being treated by other specialists, resolving outstanding issues regarding benefits, housing and family conflicts. In addition to information on issues relating to activities in the HD, a mediator is appointed to read out the minutes.

Users can also take part in the Work and Income Generation Program, a partnership between the State Department of Health and the State Department of Work and Income, through NUSAMT (Nucleo de Saude Mental e Trabalho), which offers training courses, job vacancies through partnerships with private companies and the use of patients to work in the center itself.

All the interviewees said they felt good when they were at the HD, saying that weekends were bad because they had to stay at home with nothing to do.

3 - METHODOLOGY

> There are certain men who do not command the admiration of their contemporaries, even though their greatness rests on attributes and achievements that are completely foreign to the goals and ideals of the crowd. One could easily be inclined to assume that, in the end, only a minority appreciate these great men, while the majority care little for them. However, due not only to the discrepancies between people's thoughts and their actions, but also to the diversity of their desirous impulses, things are probably not that simple. (FREUD, 1930)

Listening to the insane. To find out, from their speeches, how they understand the changes proposed by the Brazilian Psychiatric Reform. Qualitative research is believed to be the most appropriate approach for defining, as the object of study, users' social representations of the changes proposed by the Brazilian Psychiatric Reform. This would allow us to understand the meanings and definitions of a given situation as people present them. This approach is based on the assumption that the world is permeated with meanings and symbols, and that intersubjectivity is a starting point for reflexively grasping social meanings (Minayo, 2014). Discourse is an object and language is of central importance in the construction of social life.

Thus, 20 interviews were carried out with users who had previous inpatient experience(s). This interview sought to identify the subject with their socio-demographic characteristics and their perception of the service they are now attending in comparison with the service or services they have already been to (inpatient), as well as to find out about their plans for the future and the support network they have for realizing these plans. Users' answers to the interview questions were noted down by the researcher. The script consisted of the following questions: 1) Name?; 2) Age?; 3) Schooling - yours and your family's?; 4) Occupation?; 5) Residence - who do you live with?; 6) How long have you been attending the day hospital? What activities do you do here?; 7) Have you ever been hospitalized? Where? For how long? 8) Do you know what your diagnosis/problem is? 9) How did you find out about the Day Hospital? 10) What differences do you see between the Day Hospital and Hospital X (according to answer 7)? 11) What are your plans for the future?

The concepts guiding the research were those of Brazilian authors linked to the Brazilian Psychiatric Reform process. The data collected in the interviews was subjected to discourse analysis and it was thus possible to arrive at some empirical categories that were analyzed from the perspective of social representation which, according to Minayo (2014), is a set of concepts, statements and explanations used by people to understand and construct reality, and which makes it possible to value popular knowledge, common sense.

In the users' speeches, the following themes were categorized, as a result of the answers to three questions listed in the script:

Link to HD/autonomy; Plans for the future/will and Difference between internal and HD.

3.1 - LINK TO HD/AUTONOMY

The average time users have been attending the service is eight (08) years. Considering that the CPRJ started in 1998, that is, it is 17 years old, this is a significantly high number. One user has been with the service since its creation. He says he took part in the search for the site when the now-defunct Venezuela Medical Care Post (PAM) moved to the building where the CPRJ is now located (the team of professionals - technical and administrative - and CPRJ users were transferred from the PAM due to the Federal Ministry of Justice's repossession of the property at 134 Avenida Venezuela. To make the move possible, the users themselves took part).

Considering that the objective of the CPRJ is to coordinate crisis care and the assistance necessary for the **process of re-socialization (emphasis added)** of the population it serves, in an **agile** manner, with humanized, resolutive care and integrated with the other services within the CPRJ and those of the mental health care network, the question arises: where is the *exit door?* Users enter the service based on an analysis of their pathologies and their residence in the service's program area. But how are they then referred? Or rather, where would they be referred to? Should they be referred or should they stay?

One of the main objectives of the CPRJ is the psychosocial reintegration of users into the community. This is based on the proposal of a therapeutic process that does not exclude users from their social circle. The service therefore

proposes to provide the means for users to build their autonomy. By ceasing to be tutored by the institution, as was previously the case, the aim is for the subject to become the author of their own history, capable of making their own decisions.

The mere existence of the service, however, does not exclude the possibility of the logic of the asylum being repeated within it. As Dummer (2010) says about the CAPS in Pelotas, it is still a challenge for psychosocial care services to break with the logic of the asylum, with the invisible and unspeakable asylums.

> Manicomies that manifest themselves when we control a territory as if it were our own and raise the flags of our own truths, making it impossible to produce collectively, to open ourselves up to flows of deterritorialization in order to get to know uninhabited spaces, since the collective made up of differences can contain within itself forces that, when allied, have the capacity to produce the new, breaking with the instituted (...) (DUMMER, 2010, p.74)

Users seem to see the CPRJ's space as fundamental to staying well and they stay for long periods of time. One user says:

"*The treatment here is better, there are games to enjoy.*" Another said that the HD is a *"(...) therapeutic reference. It's like a nursery school for the mentally ill."* Another user said: *"I haven't been an inmate for over 2 years because here at HD they found a drug to stabilize me."* Another user, who has been going to HD every day since 2001, says he's going to *"stay here."* Yet another said of his plans for the future: *"To stay as I am. I don't want to study anymore. I want to have fun. I really like the workshops."*

The staff also seem to perceive it this way, which is evident in the words of many when they don't guide users to look for activities outside the service environment. One user, talking about his plans, says: *"If I had someone to help me, I'd study! "*.

One case in particular stands out. A 40-year-old[14] user, who also has a mental disability and speech difficulties, insistently wants to leave CPRJ. According to several technicians, the user's family does not want her to be discharged and the service welcomes this demand from the family, despite agreeing with the user that there is no need for her to stay.

It's understandable that they want to be there, since they recognize the HD and the CPRJ as a place where their needs are met. At this point, it is necessary to articulate this with the fact that the service is integrated and users have all kinds of care at their disposal, including a pharmacy that provides various medicines. However, they should be aware that, as they are there indefinitely, they may become dependent, which would deprive them of their autonomy and ability to manage their own process.

The discussion of autonomy is one of the guiding issues of the Brazilian Psychiatric Reform. Talking about and working with the concept of autonomy is difficult when it comes to the population of mental health services. What would autonomy be for this population?

The word autonomy has Greek origins, and according to the Portuguese language dictionary, it means the ability to govern oneself by one's own means. But how do we think about this with a population of mental health services? As Delgado (1992) says, all care implies a degree of guardianship, all protective services have the function of guardianship. So how can this issue be addressed in the service? An Occupational Therapist from the technical team makes an important point during a meeting: *"If the subject is here, lives in a shelter and receives his benefit, even if he comes here every day (in the HD), but comes alone and pays his small bills, isn't he more autonomous than he was when he was hospitalized for years without any activity, being supervised 24 hours a day?"*

Another related issue deserves to be highlighted. Some users say they are afraid of looking for work and losing their LOAS benefit. This can and should also be an issue to be analyzed. Perhaps the process of seeking out external activities, contact with the community and its possibilities, could be worked on together, from the moment of arrival, with the user and their family, who also, more often than not, need assistance and guidance.

[14] This user was not interviewed, but her story was told by her in assembly and in informal conversations.

3.2 - PLANS FOR THE FUTURE/WILL

In line with the previous analysis, the majority of users have no **desire** or any kind of project to improve their working, cognitive or emotional skills. Their plans boil down to *"staying where they are"*.

A 34-year-old user says: *"I haven't decided what I want for the future!"* And another, aged 57, says: *"My dream is whatever comes. I won't make plans, it never works out. Let life take me."* Another user, aged 56, said: *"I only think about today, I have no future, I confuse everything."*

Even some users who express a plan, such as getting married, don't present a strategy, a proposal that is even remotely possible. In this case of interest in marriage, for example, there is no partner to be chosen, only a vague desire, with no apparent operationalization.

One user, in her 43s, says she'd like to finish the university course she started but couldn't follow through with: *"If I can, my mind is too small, too weak. I'd like to look after the elderly.* "But when asked how she's going to go back to school, she replies: *"I don't know."*

Do people cease to exist because they have a mental disorder? As Amarante (2008) says, perhaps we don't pay attention to the *mortification of the self,* which, as Goffman (1992) says:

> (...) he suppresses the "conception of himself" and the "apparent culture" that he brings with him, which are formed in family and civil life and are not accepted by society. These "attacks on the self" result from the "stripping away" of his role in civil life through the imposition of barriers to contact with the outside world, the "framing" through the imposition of rules of conduct, the "stripping away of possessions" which causes him to lose his identity and personal security, and the "contaminating exposure" through the creation of a dossier which violates the reserve of information about his "sick" self. In addition to disrupting the relationship between the actor/individual and their actions, this mechanism causes an "imbalance of the self", since it desecrates the actions, autonomy and freedom of action of the inmate.

Their average age is 45. The reason for the absence, or low number, of strategies that favor the social reintegration of these individuals at a productive age is a matter for investigation. With this in mind, looking at the practices aimed at rescuing people from the *intrinsic madhouses*, where an absurd proportion of the population still lives in a condition of existence, this situation requires almost artisanal work to bring out what has been preserved in the minds of these people. So these people with mental disorders may only need help to become true architects of dreams, capable of creating. On their own, they might not be able to achieve this.

After all, when Basaglia (2005 *apud* Amarante 2008, p. 71) proposed that mental illness should be put in parentheses, he was showing that it is possible to get closer to the lived experience of subjects, concrete subjects, subjects of suffering. And there is a lot to learn.

As Rotelli tells us in Amarante (2008):

> So we have many things to learn: how to put in place the conditions that can reproduce a life, theater, music, words, parties, homes, sociability, the multiplication of affections, work; an activity that is an important mediation of objects, a reconstruction of the mediation of objects between the mad person and reality; the war against stigma and the procedures of exclusion within contexts; **to imagine that each of these people can be the protagonist of their story and that we can accompany this protagonism**; that each of these people needs to be associated and that we can help them in these associations; to learn that these people's families are full of anguish, but can be a very important resource; to learn to help these families to be together, to share their anguish and to be elements in the struggle for transformation; to learn that freedom is therapeutic.

(**emphasis added**)

3.3 - DIFFERENCES INTERNET vs. HD

The discourse of the users interviewed reveals a significant difference between the types of care (HD vs. hospitalization). However, it can be seen that although most of them prefer HD, there is no specific complaint about hospitalization and there are even some who prefer it, feeling safer when they are hospitalized.

Regarding hospitalization, the reports vary between not seeing any difference between the treatment modalities, hospitalization not being good, but necessary due to crises or suicidal ideas. One user said: *"Here at HD it's a treatment where you go home every day, take part in workshops, open people's minds. In inpatient treatment you take medication, watch TV.*

Hospitalization is only when you have a crisis, thank you." It is, however, seen as an impediment to activities such as going to the movies or the beach, or even smoking. One user says she feels safer because the professionals know how to act at the right time during hospitalization. This would not be the case in HD.

In HD, the majority of users also feel safe, with access to information, therapy in the event of a crisis, and they can leave, they are not trapped. They claim that HD is calmer. The HD, being an open-door service, allows users to understand the prescribed treatment, obtain information and still be in a place that doesn't represent the hardships of hospitalization. One 56-year-old user sums it up interestingly: *"I hate hospitalization, it makes me feel powerless!"*

A user comparing the types of care made a curious comment: *"HD is a semi-internment".*

We expected a speech that was more committed to the freedom and respect that exists in HD. The *intrinsic asylum* seems to be part of each of them. The institution's guardianship seems to be repeated for each of them. There are no complaints in their speech, just as there are none in their daily lives. Internment seems to be "only" about leaving the second floor of the building (where the HD is) to be on the second floor (where internment is). For a specific period. And then return to the second floor. Once again, it's important to link the users' statements to the fact that they are attending a service that is inserted into a device that works like a "small network".

Bearing in mind that rescuing the citizenship and autonomy of the mentally ill is the hallmark of the Brazilian psychiatric reform, there are many impasses to be investigated.

FINAL CONSIDERATIONS

The discussion on autonomy is a priority, considering that it is one of the guiding issues of the Brazilian Psychiatric Reform.

It is believed that the development of any intervention requires something that some health professionals forget in the process of composing their agendas: users and their demands. Many therapeutic proposals seem to be developed by professionals and offered to the user in a vertical way, without any compositional relationship with their target audience. That's why this research is so important. In fact, we agree with Delgado (2015) when he talks about the structural limits for research and postgraduate studies in psychosocial care:

> We should celebrate the increase in the number of articles. From a procedural and comparative perspective, however, it is important to note that, in the field of psychosocial care, there are a) an extremely small number of articles in indexed journals (despite the upward trend); b) few articles produced as a result of medium- or long-term research - reports of research of lesser scope and investment, or essays, predominate; c) inequality of regional distribution (reproducing the inequality of wealth and science in Brazil, more than 90% of articles are concentrated in the Southeast and South); and d) very low participation in journals in the field of biomedicine.

We need to do research and listen to the madman.

It is worth reflecting on autonomy: is this an achievable goal? Can users of mental health services make the processes of subjectivation real by redefining their relationship with themselves? After all, in order to have autonomy, individuals need to recognize themselves as legitimate subjects of rights, protagonists of their own history.

These questions persist when we look at the average length of stay of users in the service. A crystallization of bonds is perceived, which de-characterizes the process of autonomy, the target of de-institutionalization. Adherence to HD could be harmful. But to what extent?

Substitute services are seen as a means to an end, as Yasui (2010) says of CAPS:

> CAPS is a means, a path, not an end. It is the possibility of weaving, of care that is not provided in just one place, but is woven into a wide network of alliances that includes different social sectors, different services, different actors and caregivers.

In short, research needs to take place, and mental health services need to investigate the possible benefits that the processes of subjectivation and objectivation, as complementary, would bring to the lives of users, and perhaps autonomy would be achieved.

REFERENCES

AMARANTE, **P.(org) .Saude Mental, Formagao e Critica. Rio de Janeiro: Laps, 2008.**

BRAZIL. **Ministry of Health. Secretariat of Health Care/DAPE. Mental Health in the SUS: access to treatment and changing the care model. Management Report 2003-2006. Ministry of Health: Brasilia, January 2007**

BRAZIL. Ministry of Social Development and Fight against Hunger. Lei Organica de Assistencia Social: Brasilia, December, 1993.

DELGADO, P. G. **As razoes da tutela**. Rio de Janeiro: Te Cora, 1992.

DELGADO, P.G. **Limits to innovation and research in psychiatric reform**. Physis Revista de Saude Coletiva, Rio de Janeiro, 25 [1]: 13-18, 2015

DUMMER, C. A. **Praticas Profissionais na Saude Mental, Logica Manicomial e Processos de Resistencia uma Cartografia do CAPS Escola de Pelotas**. Catholic University of Pelotas, 2010.

GOFFMAN, E. **Manicomios, Prisons and Convents**. Sao Paulo, Editora Perspectiva, 1992.

MINAYO, M. C. S. **The challenge of knowledge**: qualitative research in health. 11. ed. Sao Paulo: Hucitec, 2014

SIGMUND, F. 1927-1931 (vol. XXI). **Complete Psychological Works**: Brazilian Standard Edition. Rio de Janeiro: Imago, 1996.

YASUI, S. **Rupturas e encontros** : desafios da Reforma Psiquiatrica Brasileira. Ed. Fiocruz, Rio de Janeiro, 2010.

Chapter 4

RIO DE JANEIRO PSYCHIATRIC CENTER (CPRJ): THE IMPORTANCE OF THE HISTORICAL CONTEXT OF THE GAMBOA REGION AND THE PARTNERSHIPS OF THE MENTAL HEALTH SERVICE

Erika Barbosa de Araujo

Cristiane de Carvalho Guimaraes

INTRODUCTION

Psychiatric care has been the protagonist of major discussions and changes in Brazil. Through the Antimanicomial Struggle movement, mental health has been restructured in order to meet the demands of individuals with mental disorders. The Psychiatric Reform movement proposes, among other things, the restructuring of mental health services, the deconstruction of the old model of care (asylums) with inhumane characteristics, aiming to build a new place for madness.

Thus, from the second half of the 20th century onwards, the model of psychiatric treatment and care based on long-term hospitalization began to be problematized and discussed in the Western world. Amarante (2013) proposes a periodization of this movement into 3 distinct moments: *Alternative Trajectory* - First denunciations; creation of the MTSM (Mental Health Workers' Movement); introduction of the deinstitutionalization strategy within public policies. 260 professionals are fired as a result of these denunciations. *Health care trajectory* - Decade of the 80s. During this period, a large part of the Brazilian Psychiatric Reform is embraced by the State, becoming confused with it. *Deinstitutionalization or deconstruction/invention* - which proposes a new mental health project for the country. Construction of the slogan "For a society without mental institutions" at the II National Congress of Mental Health Workers in 1987. And the beginning of new care experiences such as the Psychosocial Care Center in Sao Paulo (1987) and the Psychosocial Care Center in Santos (1989).

Ordinance No. 224/92 of the National Secretariat for Health Care (SNAS) regulates the so-called intermediate services: Day hospitals, CAPS and NAPS, which must function as local health units, integrated into a decentralized and hierarchical mental health network. Experiences of caring for the subject in their existence and suffering are beginning to emerge, trying to prove on a daily basis the possibility of building a new social space for the mentally ill. What is being sought at the moment is the overcoming of the shared consensus that the phenomenon of madness is something to be excluded from our society because of its possible character of dangerousness, (un)reasonableness and defect.

Through changes in the country's modernization policies, during the Getulio Vargas government in 1930, promoting social assistance policies, we see the creation of a device aimed at assisting those leaving psychiatric hospitals: the Rio de Janeiro Psychiatric Center (CPRJ). It occupies the building of the now abandoned Albergue da Boa Vontade, located at Praga Coronel Assungao s/n°, formerly Praga da Harmonia. It is the site of the beginning of the city of Rio de Janeiro, of commerce, the port pier, historic buildings, cultural effervescence, a bohemian hotbed, and the residence of the Imperial family. The area has an interesting and important historical and cultural heritage. Especially after the start of work on Porto Maravilha (a consortium urban operation using resources provided for in the Cities Statute, Federal Law No. 10.257/2001) urban requalification project, aimed at recovering the infrastructure of the Port Region: transportation, the environment, historical and cultural heritage, housing conditions, studies and archaeological excavations have brought to light the historical and cultural importance of the region for understanding the African Diaspora process, a socio-cultural and historical phenomenon that occurred in African countries due to the forced immigration of the African population to countries where slave labor existed (Florentino, 2009), and the formation of Brazilian society. In the mid-19th century, the region was known as "Little Africa" because it had the largest concentration of Africans outside Africa.

One of the particularities of the area today is the abundant traffic flow, where there are 3 bus terminals, the Praga XV ferry station, the Port Quay with its ever-increasing influx of tourists, Santos Dumont airport, 7 Metro stations and 1 Railway (Central do Brasil). All these factors contribute to the region having a larger floating population than the local resident population (a factor that cannot be ignored, since the CPRJ serves the population under its jurisdiction, being an emergency unit and one of the gateways to the mental health care network).

The CPRJ promotes the relationship between the individual with the mental disorder and the community, fostering the recovery of human value by offering activities that aim to enable these individuals to develop skills, allowing them to enter the job market, an integration that is favored by partnerships with commerce, industry and public agencies in the surrounding area. CPRJ aims to work within this context. Its history and work, as well as its interaction with the community and the health care network are little known, although it is understood that this is fundamental. The history of the CPRJ, as a mental health facility that cares for people who have left psychiatric hospitals, is important in the context of the Reform. Valuing the recovery of dignity, autonomy and, above all, the possibility of existing as a human being for people with mental disorders is emphasized through partnerships with the surrounding community. The establishment of interactions between users, the community and partners can favor the insertion of these (users) into the community, facilitating their inclusion in the job market and dispelling the stereotype of the "crazy" person who is frightening and cannot live in society.

The aim of the research was to learn about the history of the CPRJ and to analyze its interaction with the community. In order to get to know the institution's relationship with its surroundings, the researchers took part in community meetings, such as the residents' association and the community services association, as well as interviews with representatives of the 5th Military Police Battalion, the Municipal Guard, in the person of one of its inspectors, the president of the Security Council, a representative of the region's business owners and the judiciary, in order to observe the dynamics of this interaction.

The research was supported by the Scientific Initiation Program of the Estacio de Sa University and the ethical and scientific norms for conducting research with human beings were observed in accordance with Resolution 196 of October 10, 1996 of the National Health Council, and the project was approved by the Research Ethics Committee of the same University.

METHOD

The research "Centro Psiquiatrico Rio de Janeiro: a importância do contexto historico da Gamboa e as parcerias do servigo de saude mental" (Rio de Janeiro Psychiatric Center: the importance of the historical context of Gamboa and the partnerships of the mental health service) was qualitative, exploratory in nature, and used bibliographic and documentary research techniques. Its purpose was to learn about the history of the CPRJ, analyze the interaction of this institution with the community and its relations with the mental health care network in the city and state of Rio de Janeiro. A semi-structured interview was used to gather data, with questions to the partners about "knowledge of the CPRJ and the work it does, the existence of contact between the institution and the CPRJ, interest in expanding/creating a partnership".

INTERVIEWS

The interviews made it possible to identify the relationship between the partners and the CPRJ. These were conducted with representatives of the Rio de Janeiro Court of Justice (TJRJ), the CPRJ Human Resources Department, the 5th Military Police Battalion and the Municipal Guard. The partnership with the TJRJ takes place through the provision of services by prisoners in the CPRJ, serving alternative sentences. This partnership has existed for 10 years and is considered to be successful, as the representative of the judiciary explains: in the case of service, they try to place the convict in places close to their home or work, in registered institutions. There are currently 163 registered institutions, including schools, public hospitals and philanthropic institutions. In order to register, these institutions are visited and approved by the technical team. In the case of the CPRJ, the partnership was initiated by psychologist Luiz Antonio.

The interview with a representative of CPRJ's Human Resources Department provided an insight into the work of income generation, which consists of the development of activities by users with the aim of promoting resources so that they can enjoy autonomy in terms of income provision through their own efforts, the Social Inclusion through Work Project (PISTRABE), was created in 2012 to include CPRJ users in the supermarket sector and, in 2013, in the transport sector, with the aim of complying with the Basic Law on inclusion for people with disabilities (in this case, mental disabilities), with the basic characteristics of making working hours and working hours more flexible, while the patient is undergoing treatment, in order to minimize the stigma of incapacity and the refusal to be included not only in the job market but also in society. For this program, CPRJ's partner is Moinho Fluminense (Bunge), which donates material for the production of food that is sold and the proceeds go to the users. The partnerships with the 5th Battalion of the Military Police and the Municipal Guard, based on the analysis of the data collected, showed that they seek to have their demands met, in terms of assistance to civil servants, since the workload is often exhausting and there is a long waiting list in the network designed to assist the corporation. The partnership is seen as a useful way of resolving emergency situations. They also point out the need for psychoeducation programs and integration between the CPRJ's multi-professional team and law enforcement agencies. They report a lack of information on how to approach individuals who show "alterations" on the streets. It's worth pointing out that the partners are unanimous in reporting that CPRJ users are not a danger, that they don't get involved in conflicts with the community, and that the representatives of the public authorities mention that there are no records of incidents resulting from attacks involving users of mental health services.

CONCLUSION

Mental health service users face countless difficulties in integrating into society. After all, madness is an enigma and frightening. The CPRJ, as a mental health facility, aims to promote the dignity of users, and working with partnerships is a powerful strategy for guaranteeing the right to autonomy, to come and go, and also to remain in the spaces common to all.

REFERENCES

AMARANTE, P. D. C. (2013). **Crazy for Life**: the trajectory of psychiatric reform in Brazil. Rio de Janeiro, Ed. Fiocruz.

BRAZIL. Law 10.257 (2001). Available at <http://www.rio.rj.gov.br/web/secpar/porto-maravilha>. Accessed on September 13, 2017.

BRASIL. Portaria (SNAS) Secretaria Nacional de Assistencia a Saude 224. (1992). Available at <www.saude.sc.gov.br/geral/planos/programa_e_projetos/saude_mental/portaria_n224> . Accessed on September 13, 2017.

FLORENTINO, M. A. (2009). African diaspora. **Duetto Magazine**. Living History. Available at: <http://www2.uol.com.br/historiaviva/reportagens/a_diaspora_africana_imprimir.html>. Accessed on October 7, 2016.

LOBATO FILHO, F. S. Como Garantir Acesso, Continuidade e Integralidade na Atendimento em Saude Mental a Pessoas com Transtornos Mentais. 60 p. Monograph (Specialization in Health Systems Management) - **National School of Public Health, Oswaldo Cruz Foundation.**

Chapter 5

MENTAL HEALTH NARRATIVES: a study with users at Caps Jair Nogueira

Cristiane de Carvalho Guimaraes Juliana Caroline Mendonca da Silva Stephany Reis Vale

INTRODUCED

The start of the research

The research "Narratives of mental health: a study with users of Caps Jair Nogueira" began in February 2016 and aims to analyze, through the narratives of the users of this Psychosocial Care Center (Caps), their perception of the effectiveness of the changes that the Brazilian Psychiatric Reform proposes to make.

The research was supported by the Research Productivity Program of the Estacio de Sa University and the ethical and scientific norms for conducting research with human beings were observed in accordance with Resolution 196 of October 10, 1996 of the National Health Council, and the project was approved by the Research Ethics Committee of the same university. The project was also authorized by the Superintendent of Mental Health of the Municipality of Nova Iguaqu, as well as by the Caps technical team and its users in a general meeting. Everyone welcomed the researchers kindly and was asked to answer the interviews, as well as to find a place within the facility so that the narratives could be heard. Sixteen narratives were collected, from men and women, all with histories of long internments.

Methodology

This is a qualitative study that uses interviews as its main methodological tool. The interviews produce narratives that aim to understand, in an interpretative way, the processes of constructing meaning, the universe of meanings, the social actions and relationships between the subjects, situated in a certain context and historical moment, and the way in which they share their own experiences and their meanings. We used Ricoeur's (1994) narrative approach, which makes it possible to understand, through what users say about their experiences, the effects of these new forms of care on their lives. Just as Surjus (2007) says, this research uses Ricoeur's (1994) narrative proposition to reconstruct the untold stories of those who supposedly regain the power of speech and build their difference.

The users attend Caps Jair Nogueira, in the city center of Nova Iguaçu. The sample was made up of a group of users who had previous inpatient experience(s) for at least 3 months (uninterrupted or not) and who now attend this new service for at least the same period. The three-month period was considered sufficient for the subject to experience being a user of an institution and therefore be considered a representative individual of these two realities. Users were not chosen on the basis of their pathology. The interviewees' medical records are also analyzed and objective information, such as age, housing, diagnosis defined by the mental health team, as well as the presence of the Singular Therapeutic Project (PTS) are verified.

Throughout the text, references are made to the users' speech, identifying them by the initial letters of their names.

The history of mental health in Nova Iguaçu (or the lack of it)

Today, the municipality's mental health network is made up of various assistance devices that provide psychosocial care for people with mental disorders. It is made up of the integration of various mental health services, including basic care services, mental health outpatient clinics, psychiatric emergencies and, above all, CAPS. The municipality's mental health care facilities are: 01 (one) CAPS III, 01 (one) CAPSi, 01 (one) CAPSad, 03 (three) Mental Health Outpatient Clinics, 02 (two) Psychiatric Emergencies and 03 (three) Therapeutic Residential Services (NOVA IGUAQU, 2010).

Caps Jair Nogueira is classified as Caps III, i.e. it is a psychosocial care service with operational capacity for municipalities or regions with a population of over 200,000 inhabitants. It is a 24-hour outpatient service, including holidays and weekends. It offers clinical back-up and overnight reception to other mental health services, including CAPS Ad. The stay of the same patient in the night shelter is limited to 7 (seven) consecutive days or 10 (ten) interspersed days over a period of 30 (thirty) days.

The device works in a house in the city center, in an area with a lot of pedestrian traffic, bus lines and a train station. So far, it has not been possible to get precise information on the year it was inaugurated. It is believed to be around 10 years old.

Despite the number of assistance devices, it can be seen that the history of the network, especially Caps Jair Nogueira, has several gaps. It is not clear who Jair Nogueira was or when he began his work. The information about the history of the Caps comes from the words of users and older staff and even from the film Estamira by Marcos Prado[15] which shows, in some scenes, a visit to the Jose Muller Caps called "Caracol" by users, which predates the creation of the Jair Nogueira CAPS. Supposedly, Caps Jose Muller was "transferred" to the site where Caps Jair Nogueira is located and its name was changed. A picture of Jair Nogueira *hangs* in the entrance *hall of* the facility and tells of him as a visionary doctor who strived to heal lives and save the sick and one of the founders of the Nova Iguagu Medical Association. According to the users, as well as the staff, the house where the Caps operates was the house where Jair Nogueira lived. Although it is large, its infrastructure is not exactly suitable for users. The pharmacy, for example, as well as the application of medication, is on the second floor, which can lead to accidents. The psychology department also doesn't have a suitable location, and is held in areas of the house that don't have total privacy.

How Caps Jair Nogueira works

Caps is open 24 hours a day, every day of the week. There are 54 employees, including senior technicians and support and cleaning staff, and around 1500 registered users, according to information gathered from the device manager[16] . It is possible for up to 6 users to be in full service. At least two nursing technicians are available at night.

During the day there is information about therapeutic workshops, such as the voice workshop, the games workshop and the therapeutic workshop. Also mentioned are the assembly that takes place once a week and the team meeting. These workshops are only run by the physical educators, the psychologist and the social worker. There are no reports of workshops run by medical professionals. In fact, according to users, there is no frequent presence of doctors on site.

However, we didn't find any agenda for the workshops, although we do know that, according to their guidelines, they were sent by the Superintendent of Mental Health of Nova Iguagu to the team of researchers:

> The care provided to patients at CAPS III includes the following activities: a - individual care (medication, psychotherapy, counseling, among others); b - group care (psychotherapy, operative group, social support activities, among others); c - care in therapeutic workshops run by professionals with higher or middle education; d - home visits

[15] Estamira is a Brazilian documentary film directed by Marcos Prado and produced by Jose Padilha, released in 2005.

> and care; e - family care; f - community activities focusing on integrating the mentally ill into the community and their family and social integration (NOVA IGUAQU, 2016).

Describing users

Twenty users were interviewed, ten women and ten men. Their average age was 48. Their schooling ranged from elementary to high school, with elementary school being predominant. They reported a variety of occupations: housewife, laborer, invoice clerk, general service assistant, seamstress, mechanical fireman. One of the interviewees did not have any formal schooling or informal reading skills. They were admitted to hospitals such as Hospital Psiquiatrico Pedro II, Hospital de Paracambi, Hospital Santa Cecilia and Casa de Saude Dr. Eiras, Hospital da Posse, Clinica da Gavea, Clinica Psiquiatrica Corcovado, Humaita, Clinica Duque de Caxias, Casa de Saude Sao Jose, Hospital Colonia Rio Bonito, Amendoeiras, Ambulatorio de Saude Mental de Miguel Couto, Hospital Philippe Pinel, Clinica Vale do Paraiba and Hospital Henrique Roxo.

[16] Interview given to the researchers on 27/09/16

According to their reports, the users' support network is diverse, sometimes in the company of their parents and children, and mostly with their brothers and sisters.

Most of the users say they don't know which illness is affecting them, but the medical records show that most of them have been diagnosed with schizophrenia and bipolar disorder. LOAS - Beneficio de Prestagao Continuada (Continuous Cash Benefit) - which is essentially a welfare benefit, is the source of income for six of the users interviewed. Other welfare benefits such as Bolsa Familia and *De volta*[16] *para casa* are also part of their income. Four users reported that they did not receive any kind of social assistance.

On average, they have been with Caps for 14 years. However, this data is often indeterminate since they don't know when they started and the medical records aren't precise either.

---

[16] Bolsa Familia - This is a direct cash transfer program aimed at families in situations of poverty and extreme poverty throughout the country, so that they can overcome their vulnerability and poverty. The program seeks to guarantee these families the right to food and access to education and health. http ://bolsafamilia.datasus. gov.br/w3c/bfa.asp

Back Home - The Back Home Program was instituted by President Lula, through the signing of Federal Law 10.708 of July 31, 2003, and provides for the regulation of psychosocial rehabilitation aid for patients who have been in psychiatric hospitals for a long time. The aim of this program *is to* contribute effectively to the process of social integration of these people, encouraging the organization of a wide and diversified network of assistance and care resources, facilitating social coexistence, capable of ensuring overall well-being and stimulating the full exercise of their civil, political and citizenship rights. http://www.ccs.saude.gov.br/vpc/programa.html

Narratives

Listening to the mad. This is the ultimate aim of the research. To find out, from their narratives, how they understand the changes proposed by the Brazilian Psychiatric Reform and how these affect their lives. The methodological tool used to produce the narratives is the interview, which seeks to identify the subject with their socio-demographic characteristics and their perception of the service they are now attending in comparison with the service or services they have already been to (hospitalization).

Narratives, as Baccari (2015) says, help us to make a journey of treatment or transformation in search of a better quality of life more real. Narratives mediate between the lived experience of subjects immersed in a linguistic community and the events and temporal unity of the story told (RICOEUR, 1994). In their narratives, the following themes were categorized:

Activities

Having been attending Caps since February of this year, I've only heard of a few workshops. I've only come into contact with them at a team meeting (which happens once a week) and an assembly with the users. Generally speaking, users hang around the house, talking to each other or to the staff members closest to them. They do, however, tell us that they take part in some workshops, as user C. says. *"Writing is also living". When I have a bracelet, I make a bracelet".* Or user D. who says: *"I used to go to the voice workshop, but it closed."* And user R. who says he goes to Caps once a week and attends meetings with the psychologist. *"It's a place where I can let off steam. I like it a lot." "I'm well looked after at the meetings with the doctors".* Many users talk about the physical exercise activities, as R. tells us: *"I do physical education, clay, painting".* It can be seen, however, that some users do not adhere to the proposed activities. Their answers to questions about their activities at Caps are summarized as follows: *"I sew, I draw, I do physical activity",* but all sporadically. All of them are unanimous, however, in saying that they like to come to the Caps to talk, as C. says: *"I like to come, I come on Mondays and Tuesdays, I talk to my friends, I smoke a cigarette under the tree".* Or as another user M. says: *"Here at Caps; I just sit here, everyone knows me".*

We believe that this is a relevant issue, as it concerns a subject that is fundamental within the discussions on Psychiatric Reform: the PTS (Singular Therapeutic Project).

The PTS is the main instrument for interdisciplinary work in the Caps and enables participation, reintegration and the building of autonomy for the user/family in psychic distress. The PTS aims to create different treatment methods for each individual, taking into account their subjective demands, which is why the presence of this instrument in these services is fundamental.

> The construction of a singular therapeutic project must be understood as a strategy, with the aim of integrating this subject holistically into society and involves not only the individual with a mental disorder, but also their support network and even the social network to promote their autonomy and inclusion, as reported in the guiding document issued by the Ministry of Health "....a set of articulated therapeutic conduct proposals for an individual or collective subject, the result of collective discussion by an interdisciplinary team, with matrix support if necessary (BRASIL, 2007).

We can therefore see the magnificent proposal of the PTS, being an instrument that goes beyond the medical paradigm in the search to solve people's needs beyond the diagnostic criteria. On the other hand, in real or theoretical contact with mental health facilities[17] , the lack of organization of these facilities and the team's overload of responsibilities due to the high demand for work and their difficulty in identifying the theoretical basis of their practice in the Caps. The construction of the PTS requires the transformation of the care model and the reorganization of services, since the way they are organized can make it easier or more difficult to build the strategies planned to make the project effective. It must be centered on the user, in all their needs and context, adaptable to the changes of each moment of life and be periodically re-evaluated. The absence or poor formation of such a project means that the user will not be treated, sustainable changes over time will be unattainable and it may not be possible to reduce the subject's exclusive dependence on mental health services. This absence can interfere with the evolution of the users' treatment, as it is clear that the routine they are part of may not be having the expected effect on the goal of deinstitutionalization, which Caps aims to achieve.

We didn't see any PTS in the users' medical records. In some medical records there is an indication of the PTS, but without a definition of what is indicated for the subject. There doesn't seem to be an organization of workshops that refers to projects with specific objectives.

The PTS is indispensable in the care of people with mental disorders. The consequences of not applying it go beyond the structure of the Caps. The PTS, which aims to singularize and

[17] The study "The Voice of Mental Health Users" (GUIMARAES, 2014) also found that it was difficult to develop the PTS.

include the subject, seems not to be being done in the most appropriate way. We would point out, however, that there is an intention to promote activities within the Caps through workshops, since it is noticeable in the users' accounts of their practices. The activities and workshops proposed by Caps are essential in the process of deinstitutionalization.

Some questions remain unanswered and could lead to further research: is this a characteristic not only of this device, but of the Baixada Fluminense? How are employees prepared for implementation?

Another fundamental finding of this research was in relation to users' medical records, which were often poorly organized and mixed up with content unrelated to the Caps. The medical record is used by the institution that provides health care, as well as for teaching, research, drawing up health policies and evaluating the quality of the care provided. Various parts of a user's medical record are consulted by the different professionals who are directly or indirectly involved in the user's care. For this reason, poorly prepared medical records can jeopardize the user's treatment, as can the absence of a PTS.

Violence vs. respect and freedom

Many users report episodes of violence suffered during their stays in the various psychiatric hospitals, as user J describes - *"I was shocked, lionized, given medicine straight into the candle"*. This type of treatment was quite common in mental institutions.

> They did not receive dignified treatment, were often treated with violence and, because they were not stimulated, all their potential was reduced until they became incapable of returning to social life (ANDRADE; PEDRAO, 2005).

The madman was treated like an object, his personal needs were not met, his body was not respected and his speech was ignored. As well as physical violence, there was psychological violence, as user R said: *"It's better to live with pigs than to stay at Pinel"*. The total lack of importance given to the insane person was so overwhelming that many of them reported not even knowing why they had been hospitalized for the first time, and some couldn't remember how, when or where their first hospitalization had taken place. Some users say that they were hospitalized for problems that were not related to madness, as user J says: *"He was hospitalized because he had a stroke"*.

It is inevitable to notice the marks that the asylum has left on their lives, physically and emotionally. Many are very weak (slurred speech, tremor, difficulty walking, etc.) due to many years of taking antipsychotic drugs and the mistreatment they suffered in the institutions. They carry with them the marks of the suffering they experienced in mental institutions, which can be seen in their expressions of discontent and in their accounts of the traumas they acquired as a result of the episodes of judgement, as user D said when asked if she would like to take part in the research - *"I don't want to. Whenever I remember what happened, I feel like a little sponge being squeezed. So I don't want to"*.

On the other hand, we can see that the paradigm shift seems to have been significant in their lives. The new treatment environment (Caps) provides one of the best therapies there could be: freedom. Their narratives are almost unanimous in showing the pleasure of feeling free, as user C says: *"Here, the difference is that you're free. You have the right to come and go. Here people treat you very well"*.

> Previously stripped of their identity, deprived of their most basic rights to freedom and without the chance to own any personal belongings (the few they did have had to be carried with their bodies), these survivors are now living. They are characters in the city: passers-by on the urban scene, neighbors, workers and also tourists, students and artists. They composed and compose new stories in the world (BRASIL, 2016).

However, freedom should be seen as a greater good, but not just as the only form of therapy. The user must go through the process of psychosocial rehabilitation, rebuilding the exercise of citizenship.

Inconsistent pianos for the future

One can see in the users the absence of any kind of project involving the improvement of their working, cognitive or emotional capacities. Their plans boil down to *"doing nothing"*, as M., a user who lives on the streets of the city when she's not at Caps, puts it: *"washing the dishes, tidying the house, making food..."*. Do people cease to exist because they have a mental disorder? As Amarante (2008) says, perhaps they don't pay attention to *the mortification of the self,* which, as Goffman (2001) puts it:

> (...) he suppresses the "conception of himself" and the "apparent

> culture" that he brings with him, which are formed in family and civil life and are not accepted by society. These "attacks on the self" result from the "stripping away" of his role in civil life through the imposition of barriers to contact with the outside world, the "framing" through the imposition of rules of conduct, the "stripping away of possessions" which causes him to lose his identity and personal security, and the "contaminating exposure" through the creation of a dossier which violates the reserve of information about his "sick" self. In addition to disrupting the relationship between the actor/individual and their actions, this mechanism causes an "imbalance of the self", since it desecrates the actions, autonomy and freedom of action of the inmate.

His average age is 48. A productive age, when we should be building plans for growth, whether personal or professional. It's interesting to observe the strategies that help these individuals in their initiatives. A 42-year-old user says: *"I'd like to be a policeman like my father. My father was a vigilante". "I only want to be a MP, BOPE or Federal police officer. I don't like the other police.* Another, 50 years old, said: *"I'd like to have an apartment from the housing company (Minha casa, Minha vida)."* J. tells us: *"I want to build another house for myself, I want to do other things. Go back to work".* How can these desires/intentions be balanced? Is it possible? A police career that doesn't start when we're in the middle of our lives. A house project that isn't impossible, but isn't targeted. The plans are incipient, almost faded dreams. Alone, these individuals may not be able to articulate these processes. Let's look at the practices in order to rescue the subjects of the invisible and unspeakable asylums that are still expressed in the thoughts and attitudes of modern men:

> While it is true that the asylum as a building and epistemic space is today in a state of ruin, it is also true that as a way of perceiving and acting in relation to difference, it is still impregnated in the minds of the subjects and folded into their bodies. The notions of isolation and social exile are still comfortable, but the view of difference is generally somewhat intact, smooth, impervious to cuts and new foldings (FONSECA; ENGELMAN: PERRONE, 2007, p.9.).

We can see that an absurd proportion of the population still lives in a condition of being segregated from existence, and this situation requires almost artisanal work to bring to light what has been preserved in the sphere of these people's minds. In this way, these people with mental disorders may only need help to become true architects of dreams, capable of creating. The asylum where they were "treated" didn't allow this, because:

> The asylum is a space where time (at the same time) penetrates with total intensity or doesn't penetrate at all, it has no ability to intervene in history. Or even because there are no more histories, no more projects, where, for so long, there is no time. Time is so absolute that it cannot be relativized. At the same time as there is time for everything, there is no time for anything. (AMARANTE, 2015, p.83)

But we can (and must) change this reality in the new devices. After all, when Basaglia (2005 *apud* Amarante 2008, p. 71) proposed that mental illness should be put in parentheses, he was showing that it is possible to get closer to the lived experience of subjects, concrete subjects, subjects of suffering. And there is a lot to learn.

As Rotelli tells us in Amarante (2008):

> So we have many things to learn: how to put in place the conditions that can reproduce a life, theater, music, words, parties, homes, sociability, the multiplication of affections, work; an activity that is an important mediation of objects, a reconstruction of the mediation of objects between the mad person and reality; the war against stigma and the procedures of exclusion within contexts; **to imagine that each of these people can be the protagonist of their story and that we can accompany this protagonism**; that each of these people needs to be associated and that we can help them in these associations; to learn that the families of these people are full of anguish, but can be a very important resource; to learn to help these families to be together, to share their anguish and to be elements in the struggle for transformation; to learn that freedom is therapeutic. (**emphasis added**)

There's still a lot to learn. There's still a lot to change.

A lot of research still needs to be done and it is important to emphasize the importance of discussing autonomy, considering that it is one of the guiding issues of the Brazilian Psychiatric Reform.

It is believed that the development of any intervention requires something that some health professionals forget in the process of composing their agendas: users and their demands. Many therapeutic proposals seem to be developed by professionals and offered to the user in a vertical way, without any compositional relationship with their target audience. That's why this research is so important. In fact, we agree with Delgado (2015) when he talks about the structural limits for research and postgraduate studies in psychosocial care:

> We should celebrate the increase in the number of articles. From a procedural and comparative perspective, however, it is important to note that, in the field of psychosocial care, there are a) an extremely small number of articles in indexed journals (despite the upward

> trend); b) few articles produced as a result of medium- or long-term research - reports of research of lesser scope and investment, or essays, predominate; c) inequality of regional distribution (reproducing the inequality of wealth and science in Brazil, more than 90% of articles are concentrated in the Southeast and South); and d) very low participation in journals in the field of biomedicine.

We need to do research and listen to the madman.

It is worth reflecting on autonomy: is this an achievable goal? Can users of mental health services make the processes of subjectivation real, redefining the relationship between themselves and themselves? After all, in order to have autonomy, individuals need to recognize themselves as legitimate subjects of rights, protagonists of their own history.

These questions persist when we look at the average length of stay of users in the service. A crystallization of bonds is perceived, which de-characterizes the process of autonomy, the target of de-institutionalization. Adherence to Caps could be harmful. But to what extent?

Substitute services are understood as a means and not an end, as Yasui says (2010) on the Caps:

> CAPS is a means, a path, not an end. It is the possibility of weaving, of care that is not provided in just one place, but is woven into a wide network of alliances that includes different social sectors, different services, different actors and caregivers.

In short, research needs to take place, and mental health services need to investigate the possible benefits that the processes of subjectivation and objectivation, as complementary, would bring to the lives of users, and perhaps autonomy would be achieved.

FINAL CONSIDERATIONS Caps Jair Nogueira welcomes its users with respect and freedom. The users interviewed were unanimous in stating their preference for the Caps over their experience in the hospitals where they were admitted. Despite this, it is believed that much still needs to be done to build a new social place for the insane and to "reconstruct" their singularity. Their plans for the future are incipient, as are their personal and social organization and their integration into the community. The desire is there, as are the conditions being presented. The results of the research showed that professional practices are engaged in a movement to guarantee care that considers the user as the subject of their process, considering them beyond their status as "crazy" and without denying the expression of suffering. However, at the same time as the practices point to potential, they are still incipiently organized.

The analysis presented here is not intended to "point out" the guilty or the innocent. It sought to produce knowledge from the words of those who are most involved/interested in the psychiatric reform process, the users, so that we can direct ourselves towards the practice of caring for these lives. Living with what is different is a challenge for all of us, since we are still surprised by the suffering of others.

REFERENCES

AMARANTE, P.(org). **Mental Health, Formation and Criticism.** Rio de Janeiro: Laps, 2008.

AMARANTE, P. **Theory and Criticism in Mental Health:** selected texts. Sao Paulo: Zagodoni, 2015.

ANDRADE; R. L. P.; PEDRAO, L. J. Some considerations on the use of non-traditional therapeutic modalities by nurses in psychiatric nursing care. **Revista Latino-americana de Enfermagem**, Ribeirao Preto, v. 13, n. 5, p. 737-742, Sept./Oct. 2005.

BACCARI, I. O. P. (2015) **The narrative text in qualitative health research: methodological and instrumental references**. Campinas, 2015. Dissertation. Master's Degree in Collective Health, Faculty of Medical Sciences, State University of Campinas, Sao Paulo, 2015.

BRAZIL. **The Brazilian psychiatric reform and mental health policy**. Available at: http://www.ccs.saude.gov.br/vpc/reforma.html. Accessed on: October 12, 2016.

BRAZIL. Ministry of Health. Health Care Secretariat. Technical Nucleus of the National Humanization Policy. **Clinica ampliada, Equipe de referenda e projeto terapeutico singular.** 2.ª edigao. Series B. Textos Basicos de Saude. Brasilia: Ministry of Health, 2007.

DELGADO, P.G. Limits to innovation and research in psychiatric reform. Physis. **Revista de Saude Coletiva**, Rio de Janeiro, 25 [1]: 13-18, 2015

GOFFMAN, E. **Manicomios, Prisons and Convents**. Sao Paulo, Perspectiva Publishing House, 2001.

GUIMARAES, C. C. **The voice of Mental Health users**: a study at the Day Hospital of the Rio de Janeiro Psychiatric Center. Estacio de Sa University, 2014. Unpublished.

FONSECA, T. M. G.; KIRST, P. G. et al. **Cartographies and becomings** - the construction of the present. Porto Alegre: UFRGS, 2003. 395 pp.

NOVA IGUAQU. Municipal Health Department of Nova Iguagu. **Caderno de Organizagao da Atengao basica e saude mental de Nova Iguagu**. January 2010.

RICOEUR, P. **Tempo e Narrativa** *(tomo I),* translated by Constanga Marcondes Cesar - Campinas, SP: Papirus, 1994.

SURJUS, L.T.L.S. **Narrativas Politicas**: o olhar dos utilizadores sobre o Caps (centros de atengao psicossocial) de Campinas. Master's thesis. Campinas, 2007.

YASUI, S. **Rupturas e encontros** : desafios da Re forma Psiquiatrica Brasileira. Ed. Fiocruz, Rio de Janeiro, 2010.

No period

Reform is a process. There's no set date for it to end, and maybe it never will, because we're building a new way for society to deal with madness, and that's not easy. It's a daily, micropolitical job. Insanity has been excluded and removed from society so many times and there is a shared idea in common sense that this is somehow *natural.* We cannot allow this to happen again. Treating people in psychiatric distress with violence and rejection is no longer possible. To do this, we need to know about the work that is being done, the new types of care, the new devices and their difficulties. And these difficulties are many. It's important to reassess. So that we can improve and enhance what we have already built, together with the families, the community and all the health professionals. This is where we believe the book will contribute to the discussion.

Index

MIX
Papier aus verantwortungsvollen Quellen
Paper from responsible sources
FSC® C105338

Printed by Books on Demand GmbH, Norderstedt / Germany